THEOBALD C

incorporating The College of Law

The University of Law, Bishopthorpe Road, York YO23 2GA
Telephone: 01483 216169 E-mail: library-york@law.ac.uk

Birmingham ┃ Bristol ┃ Chester ┃ Guildford ┃ London ┃ Manchester ┃ York

THEOBALD ON WILLS

FIRST SUPPLEMENT
TO THE SEVENTEENTH EDITION

Up-to-date until October 1, 2013

JOHN G. ROSS MARTYN, M.A., LLM
A Bencher of Lincoln's Inn

CHARLOTTE FORD, M.A. Cantab.
Barrister of Lincoln's Inn

ALEXANDER LEARMONTH, B.A.
Barrister of Lincoln's Inn

SWEET & MAXWELL  **THOMSON REUTERS**

Published in 2013 by Thomson Reuters (Legal) Limited
(Registered in England & Wales, Company No 1679046. Registered Office
and address for service: 100 Avenue Road, London, NW3 3PF)
trading as Sweet & Maxwell
www.sweetandmaxwell.co.uk

Typeset by Interactive Sciences Ltd, Gloucester
Printed and bound in Great Britain by
Hobbs the Printers Ltd, Totton, Hampshire, SO40 3WX

A CIP catalogue record for this book is available from the British Library

ISBN 9780 414 032 057

NOTE TO READERS

This is the first supplement to the text. It takes into account developments up to October 1, 2013.

PREFACE
TO THE FIRST SUPPLEMENT

The Preface to the last and current edition of *Theobald*, to which this is a Supplement, opened with the words "*The law of Wills is rather like one of those country houses that have been altered and enlarge over time.*" This Supplement records further changes. Many of them might be described as routine, but necessary and important, repairs and redecoration. As can be seen, most chapters have had to be updated by the recording of legislative changes, and decided cases that have applied and illustrated existing principles. In some parts of the house, the redecoration has been controversial. For example, the decision of the Court of Appeal in the family provision case of *Ilott v Mitson* is, in our view, consistent with principle. Some commentators have, however, seen it as an unwarranted interference with testamentary freedom.

In some areas, the redecoration has involved remodelling. An outstanding example is the welcome assertion by the Court of Appeal in *RSPCA v Sharp* that the general principles by which documents ought to be interpreted apply to Wills as they do to other documents. Another example, perhaps, is the law on the requirement that gifts must be for the public benefit to be charitable.

Unusually, the Supreme Court will soon consider a case on the law of Wills. This is *Marley v Rawlings*, where a husband signed his wife's Will and she signed his. It will be interesting—and important—to see how far, if at all, the Court makes what might be, in effect, structural changes to the relevant law.

English country houses have frequently shown the influence of continental styles. The Supplement records continental influence on the law of Wills, in two respects. First, the significance of the EU Succession Regulation is explained. Secondly, the case of *Re The Erskine 1948 Trust, Gregg v Pigott*, is mentioned. In that case, the judge used the European Convention on Human Rights to help him decide on the meaning of the word "children" in a settlement. It remains to be seen whether this is the start of an important development, or merely a half-timbered duck house by the side of the moat.

We have left until last our two most important observations.

The parts of the house concerned with the formal and substantial validity of Wills, that is due execution, testamentary capacity, knowledge and approval, and undue influence, are much busier. That is to say, there are many more disputes, and much more litigation, about the formal and substantial validity of Wills. This trend had been noticeable for some years before the last edition, and it has continued. It is, possibly, the result of the spread of the property owning democracy, and in particular the rise in the value of dwelling houses. In a generation, their values have risen vastly, sometimes fivefold and sometimes tenfold.

In the context of this trend, it is unfortunate that the law relating to substantial validity is in a state of some confusion, as explained in the part of the Supplement updating chapter 3. It is difficult to reconcile the recent cases. Two things are needed. First, an authoritative protocol guiding solicitors (and other Will makers) as to how they ought to establish that the Will for which instructions are being given is the true will of a free and capable testator (in the words of Scarman J., as he then was, in *In the Estate of Fuld (No.3)* [1968] P. 675 at 719). Secondly, clarification by the judiciary (preferably by the Court of Appeal in a fully considered judgment) as to how trial judges—and lawyers advising clients before trial—ought to weigh up the arguments for and against the validity of a Will.

We have tried to make this Supplement as useful as it ought to be, and hope we have succeeded. We welcome suggestions and comments, to enable the next edition of *Theobald* to be, likewise, as useful as it ought to be.

JOHN ROSS MARTYN
ALEXANDER LEARMONTH
CHARLOTTE FORD

New Square Chambers
Lincoln's Inn

CONTENTS

SECTION E: PROFESSIONAL NEGLIGENCE

TABLE OF CASES

TABLE OF STATUTES

CHAPTER 1

WILLS AND OTHER TESTAMENTARY INSTRUMENTS

1.—INTRODUCTION

FN 2. DELETE FULLSTOP AT END OF FOOTNOTE AND ADD AT END   **1–001**
OF CURRENT FOOTNOTE TEXT:

referred to in *Marley v Rawlings* [2013] Ch. 271.

2.—CHARACTERISTICS OF TESTAMENTARY INSTRUMENTS

Conditional wills[31a]

ADD NEW FN 31a AT END OF HEADING "Conditional wills":   **1–008**

[31a] See also Williams, Mortimer & Sunnucks, para.10–15 and following.

Will revocable

FN 39. ADD AT END OF CURRENT FOOTNOTE TEXT: **1–010**

See *Drakeford v Cotton* [2012] EWHC 141 (Ch).

Mutual wills

FN 47. ADD TO FN 47 AFTER "*Kerridge*, para.6–32 and following;":   **1–012**

Williams, Mortimer & Sunnucks, para.10–21 and following;

Proof of the agreement

FN 54. ADD AT END OF CURRENT FOOTNOTE TEXT: **1–013**

However, in *Shovelar v Lane* [2012] 1 W.L.R. 637, the defendant relied on the argument that s.2 applied; the Court of Appeal described this as a "bad point". Given that s.2(5) provides that "nothing in this section affects the creation or operation of resulting, constructive or implied trusts" it is suggested that another court may well find *Healey v Brown* to have been wrongly decided.

ADD AT THE END OF THE LAST SENTENCE OF THE FIRST
PARAGRAPH:

The recent case of *Fry v Densham-Smith*[57a] suggests that the existence of the
requisite agreement can be proved by inferences drawn from the facts of the case,
rather than by direct evidence of the agreement itself. Had mutual wills not been
found, the entirety of the testators' combined estate would pass to the wife's son
from her first marriage, whom the husband disliked. The husband's own son
would receive nothing. There was no direct evidence of an agreement between
the spouses, but the Court of Appeal felt able to uphold the trial judge's decision
that an inference could be drawn from the facts to the effect that the spouses had
reached an agreement as to how to provide for the sons of their previous
marriages, and had executed mutual wills to give effect to that intention.

[57a] [2010] EWCA Civ 1410.

Chapter 2

WILLS AND CONFLICTS OF LAWS

ADD NEW FN 1a AT END OF FIRST SENTENCE: **2–001**

[1a] See *Morris v Davies* [2011] EWHC 1272 (Ch), in which an anti-suit injunction
was granted to restrain Belgian proceedings.

1.—Movables and Immovables

FN 1. UPDATE REFERENCE TO DICEY AND MORRIS. DELETE "Dicey   **2–002**
and Morris, *The Conflict of Laws*, Ch.22" AND REPLACE WITH:

Dicey and Morris, *The Conflict of Laws*, 15th edn (2012), Ch.22

FN 2. UPDATE REFERENCE TO DICEY AND MORRIS. DELETE
"22–004 to 22–010;" AND REPLACE WITH:

22R–023 to 22–063;

2.—Domicile

(a) General Principles

Burden of proof of change

FN 26. DELETE FULLSTOP AT END OF FOOTNOTE AND ADD AT END   **2–006**
OF CURRENT FOOTNOTE TEXT:

; *Morris v Davies* [2011] EWHC 1773; [2011] W.T.L.R. 1643.

(b) Domicile of Choice

FN 32. ADD AT END OF CURRENT FOOTNOTE TEXT: **2–008**

See also *Morris v Davies* [2011] EWHC 1773; [2011] W.T.L.R. 1643.

(ii) *Intention*

FN 41. ADD AT END OF CURRENT FOOTNOTE TEXT: **2–010**

Holliday v Musa [2010] 2 F.L.R. 702; *Morris v Davies* [2011] EWHC 1773;
[2011] W.T.L.R. 1643.

FN 42. UPDATE REFERENCE TO DICEY AND MORRIS. DELETE "6R–053." AND REPLACE WITH:

6R–053 to 6–073.

ADD THE FOLLOWING TEXT AT THE END OF THE LAST SENTENCE OF THE LAST PARAGRAPH:

In *Morris v Davies* [2011] EWHC 1773; [2011] W.T.L.R. 1643, it was held that a British citizen living in Belgium and working in France had not lost his domicile of origin, and had remained domiciled in England throughout. His connection with France was purely one of convenience for work. He had a more substantial connection with Belgium, but the evidence did not come close to discharging the burden of proving he had acquired a domicile of choice. Having examined the evidence, the judge concluded that in all the circumstances, the deceased "would have been horrified to learn that after his death it would be suggested in open court that he had acquired a domicile of choice of Belgium" (at [73]).

(d) Domicile of Dependence

(ii) *Mentally incompetent person*

2–014 FN 71. UPDATE REFERENCE TO DICEY AND MORRIS. DELETE "pp.160–162;" AND REPLACE WITH:

6R–107 to 6–117;

4.—WILLS OF MOVABLES

(a) Capacity

2–018 FN 82. UPDATE REFERENCE TO DICEY AND MORRIS. DELETE "27R–021 to 27–024;" AND REPLACE WITH:

27R–023 to 27–029;

(b) Formalities

Wills Act 1963

2–019 FN 89. UPDATE REFERENCE TO DICEY AND MORRIS. DELETE "6–123 to 6–126;" AND REPLACE WITH:

6–123 to 6–134;

Time factor as to content of law

2–020 FN 94. UPDATE REFERENCE TO DICEY AND MORRIS. DELETE "27–034." AND REPLACE WITH:

27–036.

Certain foreign requirements to be treated as formal

FN 96. UPDATE REFERENCE TO DICEY AND MORRIS. DELETE   **2–021**
"27–036;" AND REPLACE WITH:

27–038;

(c) Revocation

(i) *Revocation by later will or codicil*

ADD AT END OF SECOND PARAGRAPH: **2–024**

In *Curati v Perdoni* [2012] EWCA Civ 1381, the Court of Appeal upheld the first instance decision of Sales J., that a 1994 Italian will appointing the testator's wife as his "universal heir" did not revoke the part of a 1980 English will leaving his English property to his niece and nephew. It was held by Tomlinson L.J. that there was nothing in the Italian will from which to infer an intention to revoke the earlier, English will. See also (2013) 1 *Private Client Business* 2–5.

(ii) *Other modes of revocation*

FN 103. UPDATE REFERENCE TO DICEY AND MORRIS. DELETE   **2–025**
"27R–083 to 27–085;" AND REPLACE WITH:

27R–086 to 27–088;

(d) Essential Validity

FN 119. UPDATE REFERENCE TO DICEY AND MORRIS. DELETE   **2–027**
"29–008 to 29–010." AND REPLACE WITH:

29–018 to 29–024.

(e) Construction

FN 125. UPDATE REFERENCE TO DICEY AND MORRIS. DELETE   **2–028**
"27–061." AND REPLACE WITH:

27–065

5.—EXERCISE OF POWERS OF APPOINTMENT OVER MOVABLES

(a) Capacity

FN 130. UPDATE REFERENCE TO DICEY AND MORRIS. DELETE   **2–031**
"27–100;" AND REPLACE WITH:

27R–098 to 27–104;

(d) Essential Validity

(ii) *Appointment under general power*

2–035   FN 142. UPDATE REFERENCE TO DICEY AND MORRIS. DELETE "27–119 to 27–122," AND REPLACE WITH:

27–122 to 27–125,

6.—WILLS OF IMMOVABLES AND EXERCISE OF POWERS OF APPOINTMENT OVER IMMOVABLES

2–037   FN 152. UPDATE REFERENCE TO DICEY AND MORRIS. DELETE "23R–058 to 23–062;" AND REPLACE WITH:

23R–022 to 23–061. See *Clark v WWF* [2011] W.T.L.R. 961;

(a) Capacity

2–038   FN 154. UPDATE REFERENCE TO DICEY AND MORRIS. DELETE "27–023;" AND REPLACE WITH:

27–025;

(c) Revocation

2–040   FN 157. UPDATE REFERENCE TO DICEY AND MORRIS. DELETE "27R–084." AND REPLACE WITH:

27R–086.

FN 160. UPDATE REFERENCE TO DICEY AND MORRIS. DELETE "27–086 to 27–090;" AND REPLACE WITH:

27–089 to 27–092;

(e) Election

2–042   FN 171. UPDATE REFERENCE TO DICEY AND MORRIS. DELETE "27–074." AND REPLACE WITH:

27–076.

FN 172. UPDATE REFERENCE TO DICEY AND MORRIS. DELETE "27R–076 to 27–083." AND REPLACE WITH:

27R–078 to 27–083.

7.—DOCTRINE OF RENVOI

2–045 FN 191. UPDATE REFERENCE TO DICEY AND MORRIS. DELETE "4–027 to 4–032;" AND REPLACE WITH:

4–033 to 4–038;

FN 192. UPDATE REFERENCE TO DICEY AND MORRIS. DELETE "4–019 to 4–026;" AND REPLACE WITH:

4–022 to 4–032;

AT END OF CHAPTER AFTER PARA.2–045 ADD NEW PARAGRAPH AND TEXT:

8.—THE EU SUCCESSION REGULATION

2–046 In 2012, the European Parliament and the Justice and Home Affairs Council of the EU retrospectively adopted a Regulation (the Succession Regulation).[193] The Succession Regulation is intended to harmonise the conflict of laws rules relating to jurisdiction and applicable law in relation to the administration of estates and succession in nearly all of the Member States. The Regulation came into force on August 16, 2012, but most of its provisions will have substantive effect only from August 16, 2015, and only in relation to the estates of persons dying on or after that latter date. The UK has chosen not to take part in the adoption of the Succession Regulation and is therefore not bound by it or subject to its application. However, the Regulation will be relevant to the devolution of estates of UK nationals who are habitually resident in a Member State which has adopted the Regulation or who own property in such a state. The Regulation will also be relevant where the rules of English private international law direct that the devolution of an estate/particular assets is/are to be governed by the law of a Member State which has adopted the Succession Regulation.[194]

2–047 For the purposes of this chapter, the Succession Regulation makes the following provision in respect of the law governing the succession of movables and immovables, where the testator dies domiciled in a Member State bound by the Regulation:

Movables:

2–048 • The general rule will be that the law governing succession will be the law of the state in which the deceased had his habitual residence at the time of death: art.21(1). This rule applies regardless of the nature of the estate (i.e. whether the assets are movables or immovables) and whether the deceased died testate or intestate.
• However, if it is clear from all the circumstances that as at the date of his death the deceased was more closely connected with a different state, the applicable law will be that of the other state: art.21(1).

- A person will be entitled to make a declaration choosing to have his succession as a whole governed by the law of the state of his nationality as at the time of making the choice or as at the time of his death: art.22.
- The law specified under these provisions will apply whether or not it is the law of a Member State: art.20.

[193] The official reference for the Regulation is Regulation (EU) No.650/2012 of the European Parliament and of the Council of July 4, 2012 on Jurisdiction applicable law, recognition and enforcement of decisions and acceptance and enforcement of authentic instruments in matters of succession and on the creation of a European Certificate of Succession [2012] OJ L201/107.

[194] For an in-depth discussion of the principal provisions of the Succession Regulation, see Williams, Mortimer & Sunnucks, *Executors, Administrators and Probate,* 20th edn (2013), para.2–26 and following; and Dicey & Morris, para.27–136 and following.

2–049   It is presently unclear how the Succession Regulation will operate where the court of a Member State in which a person dies domiciled decides that the person was habitually resident in England. It will be required to apply English law; but it is not clear whether that includes English private international law rules, which would refer the matter back to the Member State on the basis of domicile. The answer may depend on whether the United Kingdom is classed as a "Member State" for these purposes. Where the deceased declared that his succession is to be determined by the law of his nationality, art.34(2) has effect such that *renvoi* is excluded.

2–050   *Immovables.* An English court dealing with this issue after August 16, 2015 will continue to apply the law of the *lex situs*. If that points to a country which has adopted the Succession Regulation, the applicable law will be determined in accordance with the principles set out in 2–048, above.

     This may be of interest when considering a second property located in a Member State, but owned by a person domiciled in England. The application of the *lex situs* might mean the second property is subject to forced heirship provisions. However, once the Succession Regulation is in force, the Member State would apply English law as the law of habitual residence, and it is arguable that this should exclude English private international law, and thus circumvent the operation of *renvoi* which would refer the matter back to the law of the *lex situs*. It remains to be seen how this aspect of the Succession Regulation will be applied in practice.

CHAPTER 3

SUBSTANTIAL VALIDITY

FN 1. ADD AT END OF CURRENT FOOTNOTE TEXT: **3–001**

See *Fox v Jewell* [2013] All E.R. (D) 292 CA, for how to deal with case management where there are issues concerning the validity of a will together with other issues.

1.—TESTAMENTARY CAPACITY

Test of testamentary capacity

FN 12. ADD AT END OF CURRENT FOOTNOTE TEXT: **3–002**

In *Hubbard v Scott* [2012] W.T.L.R. 29, the testator gave to the solicitor drafting the will information regarding his property which was broadly correct, but contained some inaccuracies as to its value, the extent of the outstanding mortgage and the date upon which it was purchased; the will was upheld.

ADD AT END OF THE PARAGRAPH: **3–003**

Re Key was referred to with approval in *Re Wilson (deceased)*,[18a] with the judge at first instance stating:

> "I conclude at the time the will was executed Iris was suffering from an affective disorder brought about by her deep grief at the death of her brother, combined with her continuing fragile mental state arising from her advanced age, her physical frailty and her continuing grief for her husband" (at [56]).

The judge concluded that the testatrix did not have testamentary capacity, such that the will was invalid.

[18a] [2013] EWHC 499 (Ch).

AFTER PARAGRAPH ADD NEW PARAGRAPH 3–003a:

If there is any doubt as to the capacity of a prospective testator, his will should   **3–003a**
be approved or witnessed by a suitably experienced doctor who satisfies himself

as to capacity, and records his examination: this is known as the "golden rule". In *Hill v Fellowes* Solicitors,[18b] it was held that a solicitor was generally only obliged to make enquiries as to a person's capacity if there were circumstances such as to raise a doubt in the mind of a reasonably competent practitioner. There is, it was held, no duty on a solicitor to obtain medical evidence simply because the client was elderly.

However, the recent case of *Burgess v Hawes*[18c] has perhaps eroded the golden rule still further. HHJ Walden-Smith QC, at first instance, found the testatrix's last will was invalid for both lack of testamentary capacity and want of knowledge and approval. That decision was upheld by the Court of Appeal as regards knowledge and approval, but their Lordships declined to reach a final decision in respect of testamentary capacity. Mummery L.J. expressed his concern that:

> "the courts should not too readily upset, on the grounds of lack of mental capacity, a will that has been drafted by an experienced independent lawyer . . . The court should be cautious about acting on the basis of evidence of lack of capacity given by a medical expert after the event, particularly when that expert has neither met nor medically examined the testatrix" (at [60]).

His views were shared by Sir Scott Baker.

The implication of these comments is that a solicitor's view of a testator's mental capacity is prima facie reliable evidence of capacity, and unlikely to be rejected by the court on the footing that an expert's conclusions on reviewing the medical evidence are different. Though in most cases a solicitor's view of a client's capacity is likely to be correct, this thinking runs directly counter to the reasoning behind the "golden rule", which is that mental incapacity is not always obvious to someone who is not medically trained.

The comments of the Court of Appeal in *Burgess* are strictly obiter, but have been applied at first instance, in the case of *Greaves v Stolkin*,[18d] in which Newey J. seemed to dismiss the importance of a "good social front"—i.e. that an elderly testator lacking capacity may nonetheless, on a 'good day' appear to a non-medically trained solicitor to be 'compos mentis'. *Greaves* was itself cited in the case of *Simon v Byford*,[18e] in which despite relatively clear evidence of mental decline, the judge found that the will had been executed on a 'good day' and could be upheld. Although *Greaves* and *Simon* may well be correctly decided on their facts, the editors submit that this is nonetheless a concerning trend.

It should be noted that there have been at least a dozen cases over the last decade or so where wills have been held invalid on grounds of lack of testamentary capacity, despite having been prepared by solicitors. That is itself a good reason why the Court of Appeal's confidence in the ability of lay people to detect mental incapacity is, the authors suggest, misplaced.

A degree of optimism may be taken from the most recent decision in which *Burgess* has been applied, *Re Ashkettle (deceased)*.[18f] The judge noted that the comments of Mummery L.J. "do not go so far as to suggest that, in every case, the evidence of an experienced and independent solicitor will, without more, be conclusive", and that the view of the solicitor must be based on a proper assessment of all the facts of the case, and in addition fully accurate information.

[18b] [2011] EWHC 61.
[18c] [2013] EWCA Civ 94. See also Frost (2013) Trusts and Estates Law and Tax Journal, pp.4–7.
[18d] [2013] EWHC 1140.
[18e] [2013] EWHC 1490 (Ch).
[18f] [2013] EWHC 2125.

Effect of delusions

FN 19. ADD AT END OF CURRENT FOOTNOTE TEXT: **3–004**

Re Ritchie [2009] EWHC 709: the testator suffered from OCD and paranoia; it was held to be more likely than not that she believed the allegations she was making against her children were true and that the affections had been poisoned by mental disease. The motive for the will had been to cut her children out, rather than to benefit the named charity, which the testator would not have done but for her delusional beliefs. The testator was held to lack testamentary capacity. See also *Hinton v Leigh* [2009] EWHC 2658, in which a testator had made a series of wills reducing the amount given to his adopted children, in favour of his "blood" relations. His last will gave everything to the adopted children, after he began to harbour suspicions about the "blood" relations; he was held to lack testamentary capacity by reason of delusions relating to his "blood" relations.

Time for satisfying the test

FN 29. ADD AT END OF CURRENT FOOTNOTE TEXT: **3–007**

See *Re Singellos* [2011] Ch. 34, in which the *Parker v Felgate* principle was applied to inter vivos dispositions.

2.— INTERRELATION OF THE TESTS FOR TESTAMENTARY CAPACITY AND KNOWLEDGE AND APPROVAL

FN 47. DELETE CURRENT TEXT AND ADD: **3–014**

Hoff v Atherton [2005] W.T.L.R. 99 at [62].

FN 48. ADD AT END OF CURRENT FOOTNOTE TEXT:

See also *Williams v Wilmot* [2012] EWHC 2211 (Ch).

3.— KNOWLEDGE AND APPROVAL

Knowledge and approval of contents of will

3–015   AFTER PARAGRAPH ADD NEW PARAGRAPH 3–015a:

3–015a   In *Gill v Woodall*,[52a] the Court of Appeal confirmed the correct approach to considering knowledge and approval, as asking a single question: did the testator understand (a) what was in the will when she signed it; and (b) what its effect would be. That question should be considered in the light of all of the available evidence, and the appropriate inferences to be drawn from that evidence. Lord Neuberger M.R. held that where a will had been professionally prepared by a solicitor, duly executed and read over to a testator before signing, there was a strong presumption that the will represented the testator's instructions at the point of its execution. However, this was not conclusive—in the unusual circumstances of the case, the burden on the propounder to prove knowledge and approval had not been discharged. The testatrix suffered from a severe anxiety disorder and agoraphobia. This was unlikely to be picked up by a solicitor meeting the testatrix for the first time; in all the circumstances, she had not known and approved of the contents of the will.

[52a] [2011] Ch 380. Applied in *Greaves v Stolkin* [2013] EWHC 1140.

Burden of proof

(a) *Presumption in ordinary circumstances.*

3–019   ADD AT THE END OF THE LAST PARAGRAPH:

Where a testator dictated the will (which was drafted in entirely understandable terms), both read it back and had it read to her, gave the original executed copy to the witness and there was no evidence of any beneficiary playing a part in the execution of the will, knowledge and approval was proven: *Salmon v Williams-Reid*.[60a]

[60a] [2010] EWHC 1315. See also *Re Devillebichot* [2013] EWHC 2867 (Ch).

(b) *Dumb, blind or illiterate testator.*

3–020   FN 63. ADD AT END OF CURRENT FOOTNOTE TEXT:

See also *Barrett v Bem* [2012] EWCA Civ 52; [2012] 3 W.L.R. 330; [2012] W.T.L.R. 567.

(c) *Suspicious circumstances.*

3–021   ADD NEW FN 63a AFTER "well-grounded suspicion" IN MIDDLE OF FIRST SENTENCE OF FIRST PARAGRAPH:

[63a] In *Tociapski v Tociapski* [2013] EWHC 1770, a testator's previous will split her estate equally between her two sons. A later will leaving everything to one

son only was held to excite the suspicion of the court; and it was held that in the light of the testator's dependence on her son, merely reading over the will was not sufficient. The later will was held to be invalid. In contrast, in *Poynter v Finch* [2013] EWHC 13, the entire estate was given to one son, who had cared for the testator. This was again a change to previous wills, but was held not to be a case where suspicion was aroused, and the will was upheld.

FN 65. ADD AT END OF CURRENT FOOTNOTE TEXT:

Burgess v Hawes [2012] W.T.L.R. 423. *Cushway v Harris* [2012] EWHC 2273 (Ch): a solicitor drafted wills for his elderly aunts appointing himself executor and beneficiary of one-third of their combined estate, where both testators were in poor health, had poor eyesight and where one probably lacked testamentary capacity. It was held that the gravest suspicions were aroused.

FN 66. ADD AT END OF CURRENT FOOTNOTE TEXT:

Re Wilson (deceased) [2013] EWHC 499.

FN 67. ADD AT END OF CURRENT FOOTNOTE TEXT:

Ark v Kaur [2010] EWHC 2314.

AT END OF THE SECOND PARAGRAPH ADD THE FOLLOWING TEXT:

The court will not allow the rule in *Barry v Butlin*[67a] and *Fulton v Andrew*[67b] to be used as a screen for allegations of fraud and dishonesty: see also *Ark v Kaur* [2010] EWHC 2314.

[67a] (1838) 2 Moo. P.C. 480.
[67b] (1875) L.R. 7 H.L. 448.

Mistake

(a) *Mistake as to whole will.*

AT END OF THE PARAGRAPH ADD THE FOLLOWING TEXT: **3–024**

However, following the decision of the Court of Appeal in *Marley v* Rawlings,[79a] this would not appear to be an option for the English court, as their Lordships held that rectification could only apply to a will which was valid under s.9 of the Wills Act 1837. As the wills were not so valid, the question of rectification did not arise. See new para.4–007a, below. The decision has been appealed to the Supreme Court.

[79a] [2012] EWCA Civ 61.

4.—UNDUE INFLUENCE AND FRAUD

Undue influence[98a]

3–030 ADD NEW FOOTNOTE FN 98a AT END OF HEADING:

[98a] This is a different test to that applied to examples of undue influence in respect of lifetime transactions—thus probate cases are of no utility when examining lifetime transfers, and vice versa. See *Evans v Lloyd* [2013] EWHC 1725; *Hart v Burbidge* [2013] EWHC 1628.

FN 99. ADD AT END OF CURRENT FOOTNOTE TEXT:

Hubbard v Scott [2011] EWHC 2750 (Ch); [2012] W.T.L.R. 29; *Wharton v Bancroft* [2012] EWHC 91 (Ch) (applied in *Re Devillebichot* [2013] EWHC 2867); [2012] W.T.L.R. 727; *Cowderoy v Cranfield* [2011] W.T.L.R. 1699; *Ark v Kaur* [2010] EWHC 2314 (Ch). See also *Jeffery v Jeffery* [2013] EWHC 1942, in which the will was drafted by a solicitor following a meeting with the testatrix and one of her sons, excluding the other son from the will. The solicitor subsequently sought and obtained the testatrix's confirmation that she intended to leave the son out of the will. It was held that there was no evidence that the son benefiting from the will was in a position of influence over his mother; the will was upheld; *Pearce v Beverley* [2013] EWHC 2627 (Ch).

FN 101. ADD AT END OF CURRENT FOOTNOTE TEXT:

Hubbard v Scott [2011] EWHC 2750 (Ch); [2012] W.T.L.R. 29. See also *Bennett v Petit* [2013] EWHC 955 (Ch), in which nagging by family members was dealt with as a matter of whether the deceased knew and approved of the contents of the will, and not by way of undue influence. In *Re Devillebichot* [2013] EWHC 2867 (Ch), it was held there was evidenced persuasion but not coercion; the will was upheld.

ADD THE FOLLOWING TEXT AT END OF PARAGRAPH:

In *Schrader v Schrader*,[102a] Mann J. found that the testator had testamentary capacity and knew and approved of the contents of the will, but that the will was nonetheless invalidated by undue influence, on the basis of the testator's vulnerability and dependency on her son, the fact there was no reason for the testator to want her son to have her house, evidence that the son perceived an injustice that the other son had been 'treated better'. Equally, in *Schomberg v Taylor*[102b] the testator was fragile both mentally and physically; there was cogent evidence that she was subject to persistent unwanted pressure which wore her down so that she was prepared to do what her niece said, for a 'quiet life'. There was no obvious reason to exclude her step-sons, and the will was accordingly invalid.

[102a] [2013] EWHC 466 (Ch).
[102b] [2013] EWHC 2269 (Ch).

5.—RECTIFICATION

Rectification of will on death after 1982.

FN 112. ADD AT END OF CURRENT FOOTNOTE TEXT:

3–034

See *Marley v Rawlings* [2012] EWCA Civ 61, where it was held that s.20 could not apply where a husband and wife had mistakenly executed each other's will. There was, in that circumstance, no valid will pursuant to s.9 of the Wills Act 1837; which was a prerequisite for an application under s.20. See further new para.4–007a, below. Cf. *Day v Day* [2013] EWCA Civ 280 for an example of rectification of a lifetime conveyance.

FN 114. ADD AT END OF CURRENT FOOTNOTE TEXT:

See also *Joshi v Mahida* [2013] EWHC 486 (Ch) and *Austin v Woodward* [2011] EWHC 2458 (Ch). In *Boswell v Lawson* [2011] EWHC Civ 452, rectification was refused.

ADD NEW FN 116a FOLLOWING "understood the intentions of the testator correctly" AT THE END OF THE SECOND SENTENCE IN THE THIRD PARAGRAPH:

[116a] In *Kell v Jones* [2013] W.T.L.R. 507 it was found that the solicitor had chosen the words used, such that there was no inadvertence. He was mistaken as to the legal effect of the words chosen by him, but this did not constitute a clerical error, and the will could not be rectified.

CHAPTER 4

FORMAL VALIDITY

1.—FORMALITIES FOR MAKING A WILL

(a) Signature by Testator

What is a sufficient signature

ADD THE FOLLOWING TEXT AT END OF THE PARAGRAPH: **4–003**

A photocopy of a signature of the testator was not sufficient in *Lim v Thompson*.[17a] In *Re Gale*,[17b] there was expert evidence that the signature on two codicils were forged, and one of the codicils was signed at a time when the testator no longer had testamentary capacity. Neither codicil was admitted to probate.

[17a] [2009] EWHC 3341.
[17b] [2010] EWHC 1575.

Signature by agent

ADD THE FOLLOWING TEXT AT END OF THE PARAGRAPH: **4–004**

In *Barrett v Bem*[18a] the Court of Appeal confirmed that more than mere passivity or acquiescence by the testator is required if another person signs apparently on his behalf, and that there must be evidence of some active instruction by the testator before the court is satisfied that s.9(a) is made out.

[18a] [2012] 2 W.L.R. 330.

Words following signature in time

AFTER PARAGRAPH ADD NEW PARAGRAPH 4–007a: **4–007**

Section 9(b)—the testator must by his signature intend to give effect to that will

The recent case of *Marley v Rawlings*[41a] illustrates the effect of this rule. An   **4–007a**
elderly couple signed mirror wills in which they left everything to each other, or if the spouse failed to survive him, to the defendant who was not related to them but whom they treated as their son. Their two estranged sons received nothing under the wills, but would take the estate between them on intestacy. By mistake,

each testator signed the will meant for the other—i.e. the husband signed the will meant for the spouse and vice versa. The Court of Appeal held that a claim for rectification of a "will" under s.20 of the Administration of Justice Act 1982 could be made only in respect of a valid will. Accordingly, before considering whether s.20 was satisfied, the court must first be satisfied that the documents in question satisfied the requirements of s.9. Their Lordships found that s.9(b) had not been satisfied, on the basis that the testators had intended to give effect to testamentary provisions which were very similar to the provisions in the documents which they had signed, but which were not precisely those provisions. As such, it could not be said that the testator intended by his signature to give effect to that will and the estates fell into intestacy. This decision is being appealed to the Supreme Court, to be heard in late 2013.

[41a] [2012] EWCA Civ 61.

(b) Witnessing of Signature

4–008   ADD THE FOLLOWING TEXT AT END OF THE PARAGRAPH:

It is not necessary that a witness is aware that a testator had to acknowledge his signature in order for the will to be valid; it is enough that the witness intended to and did sign a will as a witness having heard or seen the words and deeds which constituted the testator's acknowledgment of his signature: *Kayll v Rawlinson*.[42a]

An attestation clause will usually but not always provide sufficient evidence that both witnesses were present when the testator signed or acknowledged the will. In *Kentfield v Wright*,[42b] the testator's daughter alleged that only one witness was present at the signing of the will but it was held that the 'strongest evidence' was required to rebut the presumption of due execution. The will was upheld. However, in *Ahluwalia v Singh*[42c] and despite the presence of the attestation clause, there was evidence that the two witnesses signed separately, had no recollection of signing together and did not both see the testator sign the will. The will was invalid. The distinction between the two cases is the strength of the available evidence put before the court.

[42a] [2010] W.T.L.R. 1443.
[42b] [2010] EWHC 1607.
[42c] [2011] EWHC 2907.

(c) Signature by Witnesses

Presumption of due execution

4–020   ADD NEW FOOTNOTE FN 94a AT END OF PENULTIMATE SENTENCE:

[94a] Such as in *Kayll v Rawlinson* [2010] W.T.L.R. 1443, where the evidence suggested that the sequence of events as set out in the clause is not accurate.

ADD THE FOLLOWING TEXT AT END OF THE PARAGRAPH:

The presumption also applies where the document is informal and there is no attestation clause, but where there is no evidence to the contrary: *Salmon v Williams*-Reid.[94b] But equally, the irregularity may be so marked that the presumption has little force. In *Re Papillon*,[94c] the judge held that the wording of the will and the spelling errors therein were not consistent with the testator's use of language (a native English speaker) but was consistent with the use of language by the propounder (a native French speaker). The judge was not satisfied that the will had been duly executed by the testator.

In *Bhangal v Kaur*[94d] an allegation was made that the will was a forgery. The propounder of the will produced statements from the witnesses but they did not attend trial. No explanation was provided for their absence; the court held that the presumption of due execution was weakened and it was inherently unlikely that the testator had executed the will.

[94b] [2010] EWHC 1315.
[94c] [2008] W.T.L.R. 269.
[94d] Unreported, June 27, 2012 (Ch.D.).

CHAPTER 6

SECRET TRUSTS

1.—Introduction, Distinction between Fully and Half Secret Trusts, Burden of Proof

FN 2. ADD AT END OF CURRENT FOOTNOTE TEXT: **6–001**

For recent cases in which the range of the constructive trusts is discussed, see *FHR European Ventures LLP v Mankarious* [2013] 3 W.L.R. 466; *Crossco No.4 Unlimited v Jolan Ltd* [2012] 1 P. & C.R. 16.

CHAPTER 8

REVOCATION

1.—BY MARRIAGE

(v) *Civil partnerships*

ADD NEW PARAGRAPH 8–009a AT END OF PARAGRAPH: **8–009**

In the case of *Court v Despallieres*,[31a] the will contained a clause in general terms   **8–009a**
that the will should not be revoked by a subsequent marriage or civil partnership.
The testator and the defendant entered into a civil partnership some months after
the execution of the will; the testator died unexpectedly shortly thereafter. Arnold
J. held that the clause in the will was not specifically expressed to be in
expectation of a civil partnership with the defendant, and as such could not save
the will from revocation.

[31a] [2009] EWHC 3340 (Ch); [2010] 2 All E.R. 451.

2.—BY ANOTHER WILL OR CODICIL

Implied revocation

FN 40. ADD AT END OF CURRENT FOOTNOTE TEXT: **8–013**

Perdoni v Curati [2012] EWCA Civ 1381.

FN 41. ADD AT END OF CURRENT FOOTNOTE TEXT:

In the Canadian case of *Rondel v Robinson Estate* [2012] W.T.L.R. 1067, the
Court of Appeal of Ontario held that where there was no ambiguity in the
wording of the will, extrinsic evidence would not be admitted where such
evidence went to the intentions of the testator as regards what she intended to
achieve.

AT END OF THE SECOND PARAGRAPH ADD THE FOLLOWING TEXT:

The court will not readily conclude that a later will was intended to revoke an
earlier one where there is no revocation clause: *Perdoni v Curati*.[41a]

[41a] [2012] EWCA Civ 1381.

4.—By Destruction

(c) Presumptions

Will missing at death

8–035 FN 102. ADD AT END OF CURRENT FOOTNOTE TEXT:

See *Ferneley v Napier* [2010] EWHC 3345 (Ch).

FN 105. ADD AT END OF CURRENT FOOTNOTE TEXT:

See *Ferneley v Napier* [2010] EWHC 3345 (Ch); *Rowe v Clarke* [2006] EWHC 1292; *Re Zielinsky* [2007] W.T.L.R. 1655; *Wren v Wren* [2006] EWHC 2243; *Nicholls v Hudson* [2007] EWHC 3006.

5.—Revocation by Privileged Testator

8–037 FN 111. DELETE "(See Williams, Mortimer and Sunnucks, para. 16–05, fn.14)" AND INSERT FOLLOWING IN ITS PLACE:

(the new edition of Williams, Mortimer & Sunnucks also supports the view that *In the estate of Wardrop* is good law: 16–16, fn.80).

7.—Evidence if Will not Available

Proof of due execution and contents

8–053 ADD NEW FOOTNOTE FN 143a AFTER "(i) That the will was duly executed.":

[143a] In *Evans v Lloyd* [2013] EWHC 1725, a draft will was found after the death of the deceased. It was held that there was insufficient evidence to conclude the deceased had executed a will, and accordingly that the deceased had died intestate.

CHAPTER 10

WHAT PROPERTY MAY BE DISPOSED OF BY WILL?

1.—INTRODUCTION

FN 1. ADD AT END OF CURRENT FOOTNOTE TEXT: **10–001**

See cases such as *Creasey v Holmes* [2013] EWHC 1410 (Ch) and *Day v Royal College of* Music [2012] EWHC 2041 (Ch) which indicate a number of the problems that can arise, including in the former case a possible proprietary estoppel.

Joint tenancy

FN. 23. ADD AT END OF CURRENT FOOTNOTE TEXT: **10–010**

Drakeford v Cotton [2012] EWHC 1414; [2012] W.T.L.R. 1135.

The rule in Strong v Bird

FN 59. ADD AT END OF CURRENT FOOTNOTE TEXT: **10–020**

The rule was discussed in *Day v Royal College of Music* [2013] EWCA Civ 191; [2013] W.T.L.R. 591. See also *Zeital v Bird* [2010] EWCA Civ 159.

2.—POWERS OF APPOINTMENT

Formalities for appointment by will

FN 92. ADD AT END OF CURRENT FOOTNOTE TEXT: **10–022**

Breadner was referred to in the Supreme Court decision of *Pitt v Holt* [2013] 2 W.L.R. 1200.

3.—PROPERTY IN DEAD BODY

Instructions for burial

ADD THE FOLLOWING TEXT AT END OF THE PARAGRAPH: **10–026**

However, the *Borrows* (also referred to as *Burrows*) decision was doubted in *Ibuna v Arroyo*.[101a] Peter Smith J. found that the established principle in English law was that the executor had the primary duty to dispose of the body. The executor was entitled to have regard to any wish expressed by the deceased in this regard, but was not bound by them. As such, there was no room for any post-mortem application of human rights in relation to a body as if it had some independent right to be heard. In *Ibuna*, the application of this principle resulted in the deceased being buried in accordance with his wishes.

[101a] [2012] EWHC 428 (Ch); [2012] W.T.L.R. 827.

4.—CONTRACTS RELATING TO WILLS

Contract to leave land

10–034 ADD NEW FOOTNOTE 148a AT END OF LAST SENTENCE OF LAST PARAGRAPH:

[148a] *Sen v Headley* was followed in *Vallee v Birchwood* [2013] EWHC 1449, in which an elderly testator said he wanted his natural daughter (adopted in childhood by family friends) to have his house, giving her the deeds and a key. He survived for four months after the gift, but it was held that he subjectively contemplated the possibility of death in the near future, and that the handing over of the deeds and a key constituted the delivery of "dominion". At [27], it was said that equity intervenes in such cases to "give effect to the intentions of donors sufficiently evidenced by their acts such that the conscience of the donor's personal representative is affected", i.e. not solely out of sympathy for those donors "caught out in extremis". In terms of dominion, it was said at [42] that the:

> "fundamental rationale appears to be that something must be done by way of delivery of the property or indicia of title sufficient to indicate that what is intended is a conditional gift and not something that falls short of that".

5.—PROPRIETARY ESTOPPEL

Outline of the principles

The importance of context.

10–043 FN 190. ADD AT END OF CURRENT FOOTNOTE TEXT:

This distinction between commercial and family contexts was emphasised in *Whittaker v Kinnear* [2011] EWHC 1479.

Representation or assurance.

10–045 FN 198. ADD AT END OF CURRENT FOOTNOTE TEXT:

For an example of a recent case in which a claim of proprietary estoppel was not proven, see *Creasey v Sole* [2013] EWHC 1410 before Morgan J. There was little evidence of a promise or assurance, and the only evidence of the same came from the applicant. Morgan J. held there was a need to show "appropriate scepticism". It was found that the applicant had probably farmed the land on the strength of arrangements made with his parents, rather than on the basis of promises made by them to the applicant.

FN 202. ADD AT END OF CURRENT FOOTNOTE TEXT:

Bradbury v Taylor [2012] EWCA Civ 1208; [2013] W.T.L.R. 29.

FN 206. ADD AT END OF CURRENT FOOTNOTE TEXT:

See also *Suggitt v Suggitt* [2011] EWHC 903; [2011] W.T.L.R. 1841.

FN 209. ADD AT END OF CURRENT FOOTNOTE TEXT:

See *Macdonald v Frost* [2009] EWHC 2276 (Ch); [2009] W.T.L.R. 1815, in which it was found that where a testator had made no promises nor given any assurances to his daughters about leaving them his estate in equal shares, and their monthly payments to him had concerned a previous property transaction rather than the future disposal of his estate, he was not fettered by a proprietary estoppel from making a will leaving his estate to his second wife or grand-children.

Assurance must relate to identified property

FN 223. ADD AT END OF CURRENT FOOTNOTE TEXT: **10–049**

Suggitt v Suggitt [2011] EWHC 903; [2011] W.T.L.R. 1841 in which it was held that this requirement was made out.

Oral agreements and proprietary estoppel

Reliance.

FN 239. ADD AT END OF CURRENT FOOTNOTE TEXT: **10–051**

Suggitt v Suggitt [2011] EWHC 903; [2011] W.T.L.R. 1841, in which it was held that the applicant had "positioned his life" on the basis of the assurances by the deceased.

Detriment.

FN 240. ADD AT END OF CURRENT FOOTNOTE TEXT: **10–052**

Bradbury v Taylor [2012] EWCA Civ 1208; [2013] W.T.L.R. 29.

Unconscionability and proprietary estoppel

Proportionality and overall objective.

10–056   ADD THE FOLLOWING TEXT AT END OF THE PARAGRAPH:

Jennings v Rice was explained in *Suggitt v Suggitt*.[259a] The *Jennings* principle did not mean that there had to be a relationship of proportionality between the level of detriment and the relief awarded, but rather that if the expectations were extravagant or out of all proportion to the detriment suffered, the court should recognise that the claimant's equity should be satisfied in another, generally more limited way.

[259a] [2011] EWHC 903; [2011] W.T.L.R. 1841.

6.—CONSTRUCTIVE TRUSTS

Presumptions as to beneficial ownership: equity follows the law

10–063   FN 301. ADD AT END OF CURRENT FOOTNOTE TEXT:

For an application of these principles in a criminal context, see *Liscott v Crown Prosecution Service* [2013] EWHC 501.

Rebutting the presumption in cases of joint legal title

10–064   FN 307. ADD AT END OF CURRENT FOOTNOTE TEXT:

Pankhania v Chandegra [2012] EWCA Civ 1438; [2013] W.T.L.R. 101.

"Ambulatory" constructive trusts.

10–068   DELETE THE LAST SENTENCE OF THE PARAGRAPH AND ADD THE FOLLOWING TEXT:

This question was considered by the Supreme Court in *Jones v Kernott*,[318] in which it was held that on the facts of that case there was no need to impute an intention that the parties' beneficial interests would change, because the trial judge had found as a fact that they had changed. The defendant's interest in the property had crystallised at the point at which the parties cashed in the life insurance policy, enabling him to buy a new home. The logical inference from that action was that the parties intended that the claimant would have the sole benefit of any capital gain in the joint property and the defendant would have the sole benefit of any capital gain in his new home.

[318] [2011] UKSC 53; [2012] 1 A.C. 776.

Sole legal ownership

ADD THE FOLLOWING TEXT AT END OF THE FIRST PARAGRAPH: **10–069**

These issues were considered by the Supreme Court in *Jones v Kernott*.[321a] Lord Walker and Baroness Hale expressed the view that the starting point in such cases was whether it was intended that the other party should have any beneficial interest at all. There was no presumption of joint ownership, and any common intention had to be deduced from their conduct: [52].

Jones v Kernott was applied in *Re Ali*,[321b] in which applications for beneficial interests were dismissed in respect of properties subject to a restraint order. The applicants were found to be neither credible nor reliable, the applications were lodged a substantial time after the restraint order had been made, and the evidence adduced of agreement or common intention was inconsistent and not sufficient to establish any beneficial interest.

Jones was also applied in *Thompson v Hunt*,[321c] in which a couple had intended to purchase a property in their joint names but had not done so on a mortgage advisor's advice. There was on those facts no scope for the non-legal owner to rely on the legal presumption that they had intended to be joint legal tenants so as to entitle him to a 50 per cent beneficial interest. The judge at first instance had found a common intention that both parties were to have a beneficial interest, and had carefully considered the evidence and reached a decision as to the fair apportionment of the beneficial interest between the parties. There was no good basis for upsetting that apportionment.

See also *Ullah v Ullah*[321d] in which a bankrupt attempted to establish that he had a beneficial interest in properties owned by his sons. It was accepted that two properties had been purchased with the intention that he would have such an interest, but following a bankruptcy order, those interests were assigned to his trustee in bankruptcy. By the time of the purchase of five other properties, there was no longer any understanding that any property acquired would be held beneficially for him. None of them were agreed or intended to be held on trust for him, and no contribution had been made by him to the acquisition cost. His application failed in its entirety.

[321a] [2011] UKSC 53; [2012] 1 A.C. 776.
[321b] [2013] 1 F.L.R. 1061.
[321c] [2012] EWCA Civ 1752.
[321d] [2013] EWHC 2296.

Where the context is commercial

FN 326. DELETE THE LAST SENTENCE OF FN 326 AND ADD: **10–070**

At the date of writing (September 2013) the section is not yet in force.

CHAPTER 11

THE EQUITABLE DOCTRINE OF ELECTION

3.—THE INTENTION OF THE TESTATOR

Irrelevance of mistake as to ownership

ADD AT END OF THE PARAGRAPH: **11–022**

This proposition, and whether *Re Mengel's Will Trusts*[75a] was authority for it, were doubted in *Scarfe v Matthews*[75b] on the basis that it no longer represented the probable intention of a testator.

[75a] [1962] Ch. 791.
[75b] [2012] EWHC 3071 (Ch); [2012] S.T.C. 2487; [2012] W.T.L.R. 1579.

7.—THE BASIS OF THE DOCTRINE

FN 118. ADD AT END OF CURRENT FOOTNOTE TEXT: **11–035**

The ensuing commentary of the jurisprudential basis for the doctrine of election was cited and discussed obiter in *Scarfe v Matthews* [2012] EWHC 3071 (Ch); [2012] S.T.C. 248; [2012] W.T.L.R. 1579.

CHAPTER 12

WHO MAY BE DEVISEES OR LEGATEES?

2.—UNINCORPORATED ASSOCIATIONS

FN 8. AFTER FIRST SENTENCE OF FOOTNOTE TEXT ADD: **12–003**

Re St Andrew's (Cheam) Lawn Tennis Club Trust [2012] 1 W.L.R. 3487.

(iii) *Subject of gift to be held in trust for or applied for association's purposes*

FN 23. ADD AT END OF CURRENT FOOTNOTE TEXT: **12–006**

Re St Andrew's (Cheam) Lawn Tennis Club Trust [2012] 1 W.L.R. 3487.

4.—MURDER OR MANSLAUGHTER BY BENEFICIARY

The forfeiture rule

FN 37. AFTER FIRST SENTENCE OF FOOTNOTE TEXT ADD: **12–009**

Applied in *Re Murphy* [2003] W.T.L.R. 687; *Re Land* [2007] 1 W.L.R. 1009; *Mack v Lockwood* [2009] EWHC 1524 (Ch).

FN 40. ADD AT END OF CURRENT FOOTNOTE TEXT:

See Irish case of *Cawley v Lillis* [2011] IEHC 515; (2011) 15 I.T.E.L.R. 359.

5.—ATTESTING WITNESSES AND THEIR SPOUSES

Wills Act 1837 s.15

ADD NEW PARAGRAPH 12–016a AFTER PARAGRAPH: **12–016**

There is no rule analogous to s.15 invalidating a gift to a beneficiary who has   **12–016a**
signed a will on behalf of the testator at the testator's direction in accordance
with s.9(a) of the Wills Act 1837.[57a] The decision was reversed on appeal, but not
on this ground. Their Lordships did however express the view that "it is plainly
undesirable that beneficiaries should be permitted to execute a will in their own

favour in any capacity, and that Parliament should consider changing the law to ensure that this cannot happen in future".[57b] The Court of Appeal in *Barrett v Bem*[57c] reiterated this view.

[57a] *Re Lavin* [2011] 3 W.L.R. 1193 at 1213–16, per Vos J.
[57b] [2012] 3 W.L.R. 330 at 334B.
[57c] [2012] Ch. 573.

11.—MINORS

12–033   FN 106. ADD AT END OF CURRENT FOOTNOTE TEXT DELETE "para.75–02 and following." AND REPLACE WITH:

78–02 and following.

FN 111. ADD AT END OF CURRENT FOOTNOTE TEXT DELETE "para.75–07." AND REPLACE WITH:

para.78–05.

FN 112. ADD AT END OF CURRENT FOOTNOTE TEXT DELETE "para.75–06." AND REPLACE WITH:

para.78–05.

12.—PERSONS OF UNSOUND MIND

12–034   FN 117. ADD AT END OF CURRENT FOOTNOTE TEXT DELETE "para.75–10." AND REPLACE WITH:

para.78–09.

CHAPTER 13

PROVISION FOR THE DECEASED'S FAMILY AND DEPENDANTS

ADD A NEW PARAGRAPH AFTER THE THIRD PARAGRAPH:　　　　**13–001**

The draft Bill has now been published, as the Inheritance and Trustees' Powers Bill. Schedule 2 is the part relevant to this chapter, and the most important parts of that Schedule are noted below, in the text and footnotes. There may be changes to the draft, as it moves towards enactment, and reference should be made to the current position, on appropriate websites.

1.—DOMICILE, TIME LIMIT, JURISDICTION AND EFFECT OF DEATH OF APPLICANT

Domicile

FN 16. ADD AT END OF CURRENT FOOTNOTE TEXT:　　　　**13–002**

The original draft of the Inheritance and Trustees' Powers Bill, Schedule 2, also conferred jurisdiction where the claimant is habitually resident in England and Wales. See also (2013) No 4 Private Client Business 192. This provision has now been removed: see Lord McNally, House of Lords, October 22, 2013.

Time limit for application

FN 18. ADD AT END OF CURRENT FOOTNOTE TEXT:　　　　**13–003**

The draft Inheritance and Trustees' Powers Bill, Sch.2, will if enacted reverse this case, and permit an application before grant.

FN 28. ADD AT END OF CURRENT FOOTNOTE TEXT:

For a recent refusal of an extension of time, see *Berger v Berger* [2013] EWCA Civ 1305.

2.—THE TEST OF REASONABLE FINANCIAL PROVISION

(b) Applications Considered in Two Stages

Stage 1—Judged objectively, is the disposition of the estate not such as to make reasonable financial provision for the applicant

13–014   FN 86. ADD AT END OF CURRENT FOOTNOTE TEXT:

Hope v Knight [2010] EWHC 3443 (Ch); [2011] W.T.L.R. 583.

(c) Matters to Which the Court is to Have Regard

Resources and needs

13–019   FN 97. ADD AT END OF CURRENT FOOTNOTE TEXT:

The balancing of the parties' resources and needs is very much a matter for the trial judge: *Musa v Holliday* [2012] EWCA Civ 1268; [2013] 1 F.L.R. 806 (applicant was the deceased's partner, applying as his dependant; beneficiaries were his children. Appeal against substantial award dismissed).

Obligations and responsibilities of the deceased

13–020   FN 111. ADD AT END OF CURRENT FOOTNOTE TEXT:

Hope v Knight [2010] EWHC 3443 (Ch); [2011] W.T.L.R. 583 (separation agreement 19 years before death; no order for capital provision on death).

3.—PERSONS WHO MAY APPLY AND THE APPLICANT-SPECIFIC FACTORS

(a) Section 1(1)a. The Spouse or Civil Partner of the Deceased

Applicant-specific factors

13–029   FN 175. ADD AT END OF CURRENT FOOTNOTE TEXT:

For a long marriage, and the need for capital provision rather than a mere life interest and a small legacy, see *Iqbal v Ahmed* [2011] EWCA Civ 900; [2012] 1 F.L.R. 31; [2011] W.T.L.R. 1351. For a case where a life interest was sufficient where a wife had substantial other assets, see *Palmer v Lawrence* [2011] EWHC 3961 (Ch).

The "dissolution analogy".

13–030   FN 183. ADD AT END OF CURRENT FOOTNOTE TEXT:

For a recent case dealing with this and related matters see *Lilleyman v Lilleyman* [2012] EWHC 821 (Ch); [2013] Ch. 225. Schedule 2 of the Inheritance and Trustees' Powers Bill, if enacted, will in effect confirm that the dissolution analogy is not decisive.

FN 191. ADD AT END OF CURRENT FOOTNOTE TEXT:

See further *Lilleyman v Lilleyman* [2012] EWHC 821 (Ch); [2013] Ch. 225.

(d) Section 1(1)(c). Child of the Deceased

FN 266. ADD AT END OF CURRENT FOOTNOTE TEXT: **13–044**

Clause 4 of the Inheritance and Trustees' Powers Bill will, if enacted, preserve the contingent interest of a child who is adopted after it comes into force, unless the contingent interest is an interest in remainder: see para.26–065, below.

Application by adult son or daughter

ADD NEW PARAGRAPH AFTER LAST PARAGRAPH: **13–046**

In *H v Mitson*, above, the decision that no award should be made was one on appeal to a High Court Judge from a District Judge, who had awarded provision. The Court of Appeal allowed an appeal: *Ilott v Mitson*.[288a] The District Judge had not erred in law, and had properly explained the reasons for his award. An adult child did not have to show a moral obligation or special circumstances. (The Court of Appeal referred to *Re Coventry*, *Re Hancock* and *Espinosa v Bourke*, above).[288b]

[288a] [2011] EWCA Civ 346; [2012] 2 F.L.R. 170; [2011] W.T.L.R. 779.
[288b] See also (2012) 42 Fam. Law 1246.

(e) Section 1(1)(d). Any Person Treated by the Deceased as a Child of the Family

ADD NEW PARAGRAPH AFTER LAST PARAGRAPH: **13–047**

Schedule 2 of the Inheritance and Trustees' Powers Bill, if enacted, will define this category as

> "any person (other than a child of the deceased) who in relation to any marriage or civil partnership to which the deceased was at any time a party, or otherwise in relation to any family in which the deceased at any time stood in the role of a parent, was treated by the deceased as a child of the family",

and provide that the reference to a family includes a family in which the deceased was the only member (apart from the applicant).

(f) Section 1(1)(e). Any Dependant of the Deceased

ADD NEW PARAGRAPH AFTER LAST PARAGRAPH: **13–049**

Schedule 2 of the Inheritance and Trustees' Powers Bill, if enacted, will provide that "a person is to be treated as being maintained by the deceased (wholly or partly, as the case may be) only if the deceased was making a substantial contribution in money or money's worth towards the reasonable needs of that person, other than a contribution made for full valuable consideration pursuant to an arrangement of a commercial nature".

Extent, basis and duration of assumption of responsibility

13–055   ADD NEW PARAGRAPH AT END OF THE PARAGRAPH:

Schedule 2 of the Inheritance and Trustees' Powers Bill, if enacted, will reword subs.3(3) and (4), which relate to the assumption of responsibility.

4.—ORDERS WHICH THE COURT MAY MAKE

(a) The Net Estate

Property included if court so orders

13–059   ADD NEW PARAGRAPH AFTER THIRD PARAGRAPH:

Schedule 2 of the Inheritance and Trustees' Powers Bill, if enacted, will provide that the value of the deceased's severable share of the property is to be taken as the value that the share would have had at the date of the hearing, had the share been severed immediately before the deceased's death, unless the court orders a valuation as at a different date.

(b) Forms of Provision Ordered for Applicant

Lump-sum payment

13–061   FN 383. ADD AT END OF CURRENT FOOTNOTE TEXT:

Such a "clean break" order may be especially appropriate where the relationship between the applicant and the beneficiaries has broken down: *Lilleyman v Lilleyman* [2012] EWHC 821 (Ch); [2013] Ch. 225.

Settlement of property

13–063   FN 388. ADD AT END OF CURRENT FOOTNOTE TEXT:

Re Evans, decd.; Cattle v Evans [2011] EWHC 945 (Ch); [2011] 2 F.L.R. 843; [2011] W.T.L.R. 947.

Variation of civil partnership settlement

13–066   ADD NEW PARAGRAPH AT END OF FIRST PARAGRAPH:

Schedule 2 of the Inheritance and Trustees' Powers Bill, if enacted, will give the court power to make another form of order, namely an order varying for the applicant's benefit the trusts on which the deceased's estate is held.

(c) Other Terms and Effect of Order

Consequential and supplemental provision giving effect to order

FN 400. ADD AT END OF CURRENT FOOTNOTE TEXT: **13–068**

Schedule 2 of the Inheritance and Trustees' Powers Bill, if enacted, will provide that in assessing for the purposes of an order the extent (if any) to which the net estate is reduced by any debts or liabilities, including inheritance tax paid or payable out of the estate, the court may assume that the order has already been made.

(d) Interim Order

Requirements

FN 416. ADD AT END OF CURRENT FOOTNOTE TEXT: **13–073**

Smith v Smith [2011] EWHC 2133 (Ch); [2012] 2 F.L.R. 230 (application refused because no immediate need).

6.—Procedure

Compromise

FN 487. ADD AT END OF CURRENT FOOTNOTE TEXT: **13–100/1**

(2013) 3 *Private Client Business* 113.

Costs

FN 490. ADD AT END OF CURRENT FOOTNOTE TEXT: **13–102**

For a case where costs followed the event despite late disclosure by the successful applicant of a fact in his favour, see *Thomas v Jeffery* [2012] EWCA Civ 693; [2013] W.T.L.R. 141. The court can disallow a proportion of the costs awarded to signify its disapproval of a "no holds barred" approach in litigation under the Act: *Lilleyman v Lilleyman (Costs)* [2012] EWHC 1056 (Ch); [2012] 1 W.L.R. 2801. See (2012) 42 Fam. Law 1246.

CHAPTER 14

ADMISSIBILITY OF EVIDENCE AS AN AID TO CONSTRUCTION

FN 2. ADD AT END OF CURRENT FOOTNOTE TEXT: **14–001**

Parkinson v Fawdon [2009] EWHC 1953 (Ch) now reported at [2010] W.T.L.R. 79.

1.—ADMISSIBILITY OF DIRECT EXTRINSIC EVIDENCE

(a) Extrinsic Evidence Admissible on Death After 1982

(ii) *Ambiguous on its face*

FN 14. ADD AT END OF CURRENT FOOTNOTE TEXT: **14–004**

A similar case to *Re Williams* is *Spurling v Broadhurst* [2012] EWHC 2883 (Ch); [2012] W.T.L.R. 1813.

The incapable meaning rule

DELETE SECOND SENTENCE IN THE FIRST PARAGRAPH AND   **14–007**
REPLACE WITH THE FOLLOWING TEXT:

Traditionally, such evidence alone could not make words in a will bear a meaning which on the face of the will they are incapable of meaning (making "black" mean "white"),[23] although in the light of *RSPCA v Sharp*[23a] (considered further at paragraph 15–003a below) and its reference to the modern approach to construction derived from *Mannai Investment Co Ltd v Eagle Star Life Assurance Co Ltd*[23b] (where Lord Hoffmann held that 'allegory' could be interpreted as 'alligator' after Sheridan's Mrs Malaprop), this rule may no longer hold sway. In *Ashcroft v Barnsdale*,[23c] a reference in a deed of variation to cl.6 was construed as a reference to cl.5, so that rectification was not necessary, being an obvious error.

Extrinsic evidence can certainly put a meaning on a meaningless part of a will.

[23] See below, paras 14–028, 15–014.
[23a] [2010] EWCA Civ 1474; [2011] 1 W.L.R. 980.

[23b] [1997] A.C. 749.

[23c] [2010] EWHC 1948 (Ch); [2010] W.T.L.R. 1675; 13 I.T.ELR. 513.

(b) Direct Extrinsic Evidence of Testator's Intention on Death Before 1983

Distinction between direct and circumstantial extrinsic evidence

14–010   ADD NEW FOOTNOTE 41a AT END OF LAST SENTENCE OF PARAGRAPH:

[41a] This paragraph was applied with approval in *Scarfe v Matthews* [2012] EWHC 3071 (Ch); [2012] S.T.C. 2487; [2012] W.T.L.R. 1579.

2.—OTHER EVIDENCE ADMISSIBLE

(a) The Will

Punctuation and spacing

14–017   FN 92. ADD AT END OF CURRENT FOOTNOTE TEXT:

A distinction cited in *Spurling v Broadhurst* [2012] EWHC 2883 (Ch); [2012] W.T.L.R. 1813 at [24].

(c) Circumstantial Extrinsic Evidence Admissible under Armchair Principle

The Armchair Principle

14–027   FN 123. ADD AT END OF CURRENT FOOTNOTE TEXT:

See dictum of Blackburn J. in *Grant v Grant* (1870) 2 P.&D. 8; L.R. 5 C.P. 380 cited in *Howard v Howard-Lawson* [2012] EWCA Civ 6; [2012] W.T.L.R. 617.

The incapable meaning rule

14–028   REMOVE WORD "However" AND ADD TO BEGINNING OF PARAGRAPH:

For the modern limits to this doctrine, see paragraph 14–007 above. Subject thereto, the traditional rule has been that [...]

Testator's relations with claimants

14–030   FN 143. ADD AT END OF CURRENT FOOTNOTE TEXT:

Parkinson v Fawdon [2009] EWHC 1953 (Ch) now reported at [2010] W.T.L.R. 79.

CHAPTER 15

GENERAL PRINCIPLES OF CONSTRUCTION

FN 1. ADD AT END OF CURRENT FOOTNOTE TEXT: **15–001**

For a recent summary of the similar approach adopted in Canada, see *Re Thiemer dec'd* [2012] BCSC 629; (2012) 14 I.T.E.L.R. 991 at [44] onwards.

(a) The Testator's Intention as Expressed in his Will

ADD NEW FOOTNOTE 10a AT END OF LAST SENTENCE OF THIRD **15–003**
PARAGRAPH:

[10a] This paragraph was cited with approval in *Scarfe v Matthews* [2012] EWHC 3071 (Ch); [2012] S.T.C. 2487; [2012] W.T.L.R. 1579.

ADD NEW PARAGRAPH 15–003a AFTER 15–003: **15–003a**

The important case of *RSPCA v Sharp*,[10b] has made clear that the interpretation of wills follows the same principles as the interpretation of contracts and other documents, as set out by the House of Lords in *Mannai Investment Co Ltd v Eagle Star Life Assurance Co Ltd*,[10c] *Investors Compensation Scheme Ltd v West Bromwich Building Society*[10d] and presumably also of the Supreme Court in *Rainy Sky SA v Kookmin Bank*,[10e] namely that:

> "the exercise of construction is essentially one unitary exercise in which the court must consider the language used and ascertain what a reasonable person, that is a person who has all the background knowledge which would reasonably have been available to the parties in the situation in which they were in at the time of the contract, would have understood the parties to have meant. In doing so, the court must have regard to all the relevant surrounding circumstances."[10f]

There is considerable force in such a view; in *Mannai Investments* itself (at pages 778 to 779), Lord Hoffmann refers to the tendency of the courts to exclude oral evidence of what he called the background facts in will construction, to promote certainty at the expense of individual justice, with regret (although he does not refer to s.21 of the Administration of Justice Act 1982 or the common ground between his approach and that of the House of Lords in *Perrin v Morgan*[10g]).

The quotation from *Rainy Sky* above continues by saying that, "If there are two possible constructions, the court is entitled to prefer the construction which is consistent with business common sense and to reject the other". In the context of wills, it may be that the concept of 'business common sense' can be replaced by the presumptions against caprice and partial intestacy, and notions of tax planning (as in *RSPCA v Sharp* itself).

As seen above (para.15–001), the long-held view that the construction of one will is no guide to the construction of another, combined with the admissibility of extrinsic evidence under s.21 of the Administration of Justice Act 1982, already means that much of the analysis in the remaining chapters of this Section of this book may be of limited assistance. On one view, if this approach to the construction of wills gathers support, the usefulness of commentary such as this will continue to decline. However, in our view, the rules on the admissibility of extrinsic evidence in the construction of wills must continue to apply as they have been put on a statutory footing; subject to those, the interpretation of wills has been in accordance with the modern approach to the construction of other documents outlined above since *Perrin v Morgan*. Indeed, in *Thomas v Kent*[10h] Chadwick L.J. identified the 'armchair principle' (see para.14–027 above) with the approach to construction endorsed by *Investors Compensation Scheme Ltd v West Bromwich Building Society.*[10i]

[10b] [2010] EWCA Civ 1474; [2011] 1 W.L.R. 980; [2011] W.T.L.R. 311 at [22], per Patten L.J. and [31] per Lord Neuberger M.R., along with a number of other cases (*Thomas v Kent* [2006] EWHC 1485 (Ch); [2007] W.T.L.R. 177; *Rainbird v Smith* [2012] EWHC 4276 (Ch)).
[10c] [1997] A.C. 749.
[10d] [1998] 1 W.L.R. 896 (especially at p.912).
[10e] [2011] UKSC 50; [2011] 1 W.L.R. 2900.
[10f] Per Lord Clarke at [21].
[10g] [1943] A.C. 399.
[10h] [2006] EWHC 1485 (Ch); [2007] W.T.L.R. 177 at [17].
[10i] [1998] 1 WLR 896.

Speculation: The court cannot rewrite a will

15–004   FN 14. ADD AT END OF CURRENT FOOTNOTE TEXT:

See also *Webb v Oldfield* [2010] EWHC 3469 (Ch); *Rondel v Robinson Estate* [2012] W.T.L.R. 1067; 14 I.T.E.L.R. 349 (Ontario).

FNN 15–16. ADD AT END OF CURRENT FOOTNOTE TEXT:

This citation of *Re Bailey* was referred to and applied in *Beard v Shadler* [2011] EWHC 114 (Ch); [2011] W.T.L.R. 1147.

Speculation: The court does not guess the testator's intention

FN 20. DELETE CURRENT FOOTNOTE TEXT AND REPLACE WITH   **15–005**
FOLLOWING TEXT:

Such as *Allsop, Re* [1968] Ch. 39, per Lord Denning M.R.; and more recently
Blech v Blech [2002] W.T.L.R. 483; *Esson v Esson* [2009] EWHC 3045 (Ch); and
Scarfe v Matthews [2012] EWHC 3071 (Ch); [2012] S.T.C. 2487; [2012]
W.T.L.R. 1579.

(b) Presumption Words to be Given Their Ordinary Meaning

FN 21. ADD AT END OF CURRENT FOOTNOTE TEXT: **15–006**

Re Kung (2013) 15 I.T.E.L.R. 948. In *Ashcroft v Barnsdale* [2010] EWHC 1948
(Ch); [2010] W.T.L.R. 1675; 13 I.T.ELR. 513, a reference to cl.6 was construed
as a reference to cl.5, so that rectification was not necessary, being an obvious
error.

(c) Presumption Technical Words to be Given Their Technical Meaning

ADD AT END OF PARAGRAPH: **15–017**

This 'rule' appears to some extent to survive *RSPCA v Sharp*[52a] where at [22]
Patten L.J. treats the fact a will was professionally drafted as a relevant consideration. Similarly, that the testator of a homemade will is clearly fluent and
literate and in educated handwriting may indicate a more precise use of language:
Public Trustee v Butler.[52b] However, to refer to it as a presumption may be
overstating its importance, which will depend on the circumstances. See also *Re
Kung.*[52c]

[52a] [2010] EWCA Civ 1474; [2011] 1 W.L.R. 980 (considered above at par-
a.15–003).
[52b] [2012] EWHC 858 (Ch); [2012] W.T.L.R. 1043 at [11].
[52c] (2013) 15 I.T.E.L.R. 948.

(d) The Will is to be Read as a Whole

ADD AFTER FIRST SENTENCE: **15–025**

There is no priority between gifts to be derived from the order in which they
appear in the will: *RSPCA v Sharp.*[68a] See also *Re Kung.*[68b]

[68a] [2010] EWCA Civ 1474; [2011] 1 W.L.R. 980; [2011] W.T.L.R. 311 at [36]
to [37] *per* Lord Neuberger of Abbotsbury, citing the cases noted at paragraph
34–015 below.
[68b] (2013) 15 I.T.E.L.R. 948.

(e) Relevance of Extrinsic Evidence in Applying Principles of Construction

(d) *Description of object or subject of gift.*

15–033   FN 96. ADD TO CURRENT FOOTNOTE TEXT AFTER CASE CITATION FOR *National Society for the Prevention of Cruelty to Children v Scottish National Society for the Prevention of Cruelty to Children*:

This judgment was cited with approval in *Mannai Investment Co Ltd v Eagle Star Life Assurance* [1997] A.C. 749 at 778.

Chapter 16

ALTERING AND REVOKING GIFTS

ADD AT END OF PARAGRAPH: **16–001**

The principles explained in this chapter are, in the light of the admissibility of extrinsic evidence as described in Chapter 14, and following the modern approach to interpretation of documents explained in paragraph 15–003a above, only rules of last resort. They will never operate to frustrate the clear intentions of the testator.

3.—Uncertainty

FN 29. ADD AT END OF CURRENT FOOTNOTE TEXT: **16–006**

There is a general principle that the court will strive to give effect to a document that is a compromise of uncertain or disputed rights: *Rafferty v Philp* [2011] EWHC (Ch) 709; this is unlikely to be relevant to testamentary documents.

4.—Express and Implied Revocation

Revocation conditional upon gift in later instrument taking effect

(i) *Intention to revoke as clear as original gift.*

FN 77. ADD AT END OF CURRENT FOOTNOTE TEXT: **16–014**

Westland v Lilis [2003] EWHC 1669 (Ch).

FN 79. ADD AT END OF CURRENT FOOTNOTE TEXT:

This was described as a 'particularly strong case' (in the sense, one presumes, of 'harsh') in *Westland v Lilis* [2003] EWHC 1669 (Ch) at [41].

CHAPTER 21

GIFTS FOR CHARITABLE PURPOSES

1.—INTRODUCTION

FN 2. ADD AT END OF CURRENT FOOTNOTE TEXT: **21–001**

See now 2011 Act s.4, 15, 16, and 20. For public benefit, see *Independent Schools Council v Charity Commission* [2012] Ch. 214, and the amended guidance issued by the Charity Commission as a result of that decision.

FN 3. ADD AT END OF CURRENT FOOTNOTE TEXT:

See now 2011 Act ss.13 to 16, 20, 316, 317, and 318.

ADD NEW PARAGRAPH AFTER THE SECOND PARAGRAPH:

The Charities Act 2011 has consolidated the Charities Act 2006, the Charities Act 1993, and some other legislation relating to charities. See below for updating of specific references to the sections of the former Acts.

FN 4. ADD AT END OF CURRENT FOOTNOTE TEXT: **21–002**

As well as updated guidance on public benefit, the website contains detailed guidance on fundraising; land and property; managing a charity; money and accounts; protecting a charity; registering a charity; trustees, staff and volunteers; working with other organisations; and specific types of charity.

2.—THE ADVANTAGES AND SCOPE OF CHARITY

Registration

FN 29. ADD AT END OF CURRENT FOOTNOTE TEXT: **21–005**

See now 2011 Act ss.36, 37.

FN 30. ADD AT END OF CURRENT FOOTNOTE TEXT:

See now 2011 Act s.37(1).

3.—CHARITABLE PURPOSES

(a) Prevention or Relief of Poverty

Gifts to poor relations or poor employees

21–013   ADD AT END OF THE PARAGRAPGH:

They also appear to have survived the 2011 Act: *A-G v Charity Commission* [2012] W.T.L.R. 977; (2012) 142 *Trusts and Estates Law and Tax Journal* December 4.

(b) The Advancement of Education

Schools

21–015   ADD AT END OF THE PARAGRAPGH:

The Upper Tribunal has now clarified the application of the requirement, in *Independent Schools Council v Charity Commission*.[99a] There must be more than a token benefit to the public, but once that threshold was reached, what the trustees decide to do in the running of a school is entirely up to them.

[99a] [2012] Ch. 214.

Particular doctrines

21–020   FN 125. ADD AT END OF CURRENT FOOTNOTE TEXT:

See now 2011 Act s.3(2).

(c) The Advancement of Religion

Limit of religious charity

21–032   FN 195. ADD AT END OF CURRENT FOOTNOTE TEXT:

The court cannot determine matters that are simply ones of religious doctrine and practice alone: *Khaira v Shergill* [2012] W.T.L.R. 1795.

(e) The Advancement of Citizenship or Community Development

21–034   FN 216. ADD AT END OF CURRENT FOOTNOTE TEXT:

Helena Partnership v Revenue and Customs and A-G [2012] W.T.L.R. 1519.

(m) Any Other of The Purposes Listed in s.2(4) of the 2006 Act

21–042   FN 243. INSERT BEFORE "[2006] W.T.L.R. 1053"

Re Restorative Justice Consortium Ltd

ADD NEW PARAGRAPH AFTER THE PARAGRAPH:

It remains the law that to be charitable as beneficial to the community a purpose has to be within the spirit and intendment of the preamble to the Charitable Uses Act 1601, and not every object of public general utility is necessarily charitable: *Helena Partnership v Revenue and Customs and A-G.*[243a]

[243a] [2012] WTLR 1519.

FN 248. ADD AT END OF CURRENT FOOTNOTE TEXT: **21–043**

See now 2011 Act ss.4, 5.

7.—THE CY-PRÈS DOCTRINE

(a) Gifts to Institutions

Gifts to institutions which cease to exist after testator's death

FN 348. ADD AT END OF CURRENT FOOTNOTE TEXT: **21–059**

Re ARMS (Multiple Sclerosis Research) Ltd [1997] 1 W.L.R. 877; *Kings v Bultitude* [2010] W.T.L.R. 1571; *Phillips v RSPB* [2012] W.T.L.R. 891; *In the Estate of Longman* [2012] W.T.L.R. 1421.

(b) Gifts for Charitable Purposes

Failure of purpose ab initio

FN 352. ADD AT END OF CURRENT FOOTNOTE TEXT: **21–061**

Kings v Bultitude [2010] W.T.L.R. 1571.

(c) The Charities Acts 1960, 1993 and 2006

FN 370. ADD AT END OF CURRENT FOOTNOTE TEXT: **21–067**

Subsequent legislation does not affect this.

FN 375. ADD AT END OF CURRENT FOOTNOTE TEXT: **21–068**

See now 2011 Act s.64(2) and s.28.

FN 385. ADD AT END OF CURRENT FOOTNOTE TEXT:

See now 2011 Act s.64(1).

FN 386. ADD AT END OF CURRENT FOOTNOTE TEXT:

See now 2011 Act s 64(2).

FN 387. ADD AT END OF CURRENT FOOTNOTE TEXT:

See now 2011 Act s.63(3) to (7).

CHAPTER 22

RESIDUARY GIFTS AND PARTIAL INTESTACY

1.—LAPSE

(b) Wills Act 1837 s.33: Gifts to Testator's Issue

FN 42. DELETE FOOTNOTE. 22–014

ADD AFTER THIRD PARAGRAPH:

As to whether a contrary intention is shown, it was held in *Rainbird v Smith*[52a] that the words "such of my daughters [who were then named] as shall survive me" and "if more than one in equal shares" were sufficient to exclude the operation of s.33, and were not even sufficiently ambiguous to admit extrinsic evidence under s.21 of the Administration of Justice Act 1982. It was also held in *Rainbird* that extrinsic evidence under that section could in principle be admissible to determine the application of s.33. In this the deputy judge differed from the view expressed in *Hawkins on the Construction of Wills* at 24–12, that the words 'appears by the will' excludes extrinsic evidence, holding that the will means the will as properly construed, *i.e.* in the light of admissible evidence. We respectfully prefer the learned Judge's view on this point. The question of whether a contrary intention can be gathered from a will, as the opposite conclusion had been reached in *Ling v Ling*,[52b] where similar words had been used save that the children were not named and so it was a class gift.

[52a] [2012] EWHC 4276 (Ch).
[52b] [2002] W.T.L.R. 553.

3.—ACCELERATION

REPLACE THE FIRST PARAGRAPH WITH THE FOLLOWING TEXT 22–022
(FOOTNOTES: 120, 121, 122 REMAIN THE SAME; ADD NEW
FOOTNOTE 122a):

Where the tenant for life is incapable of taking a devise,[120] or bequest,[121] a remainder that is vested in interest is accelerated and takes effect in possession immediately. The gift in remainder is construed as a gift taking effect on the death of the first taker or on any earlier failure or determination of his interest.[122]

"Thus the rule is, as ever, a question of construction and must give way to a contrary intention.[122a] If the gift in remainder is expressed to take effect "after the death" of the first taker, this does not prevent acceleration unless by his will the testator has shown an intention that the remainderman is to take nothing until after the death of the first taker.[123]

[122a] See *Re Sadick; da Silva v HSBC Trustee (Hong Kong) Ltd* [2009] HKCU 1957; [2010] W.T.L.R. 863.

Effect of acceleration on class–closing

22–023   DELETE LAST SENTENCE OF PARAGRAPH AND ADD AT END (KEEP FOOTNOTE 141):

As explained below, the approach of the English courts is that a release or disclaimer of his life estate by A does not affect the composition of the class.[141]

4.—WHAT IS A RESIDUARY GIFT?

22–024   FN 145. DELETE FOOTNOTE TEXT AND REPLACE WITH FOLLOWING TEXT:

For example, *RSPCA v Sharp* [2010] EWCA Civ 1474; [2011] 1 W.L.R. 980; [2011] W.T.L.R. 311 reversing the decision at first instance [2010] EWHC 268 (Ch); [2010] W.T.L.R. 855. See also (2011) Private Client Business 95; (2011) 9 Trust Quarterly Review issue 3 (Sept) 13; issue 4 (Dec) 9.

5.—WHAT PASSES UNDER A RESIDUARY GIFT

Revocation of a share of residue

22–039   FN 208. ADD AT END OF CURRENT FOOTNOTE TEXT:

Cf. Westland v Lilis [2003] EWHC 1669 (Ch), where this result was avoided by a generous construction of the word 'fail' in a cross-accruer clause. None of the cases here noted were cited to the judge.

8.—PARTIAL INTESTACY

22–046   FN 231. DELETE FOOTNOTE TEXT AND REPLACE WITH FOLLOWING TEXT:

See generally Parry and Kerridge, 2–44 and following.

Administration of Estates Act 1925

FN 233. DELETE FOOTNOTE TEXT AND REPLACE WITH   **22–047**
FOLLOWING TEXT:

See for example Williams Mortimer & Sunnucks, 82–12 and following; Sherrin
& Bonehill, generally.

Presumption against intestacy

FN 274. ADD AT END OF CURRENT FOOTNOTE TEXT: **22–057**

Westland v Lilis [2003] EWHC 1669 (Ch).

FN 275. ADD AT END OF CURRENT FOOTNOTE TEXT:

See also *Public Trustee v Butler* [2012] EWHC 858 (Ch); [2012] W.T.L.R. 1043
at [10]–[12] where a clause was construed as creating a power not imposing a
trust of income so that unappointed income passed on a partial intestacy.

CHAPTER 23

DESCRIPTION OF THINGS

1.—GENERAL

(a) Date From Which the Will Speaks as to the Subject Matter of Gifts

(i) *Prima facie a will speaks from death*

General legacy

REMOVE "However," AT END OF PARAGRAPH.   **23–004**

(iv) *Effect of republication*

REPLACE FIRST TWO SENTENCES OF PRACTICE NOTE WITH THE   **23–011**
FOLLOWING:

Practice Note: Whenever a testator wishes to leave a specific legacy or bequest, the drafter should discuss the possibility of the subject matter being disposed of or changed prior to death, and ascertain the testator's intentions. Any contrary intention can then be made plain in the will.

(b) Wrong Description

(i) *Falsa Demonstratio non nocet*

ADD AT END OF LAST PARAGRAPH: **23–012**

In Australia, a gift of a proprietary interest in a retirement village was valid even though the testator had only a personal right under a contract in relation to that accommodation: *Re Blake.*[64a]

[64a] [2009] VSC 184.

Property testator thinks he has but has not

FN 72. ADD AT END OF CURRENT FOOTNOTE TEXT: **23–015**

Cf. the more forgiving approach in Australia in *Ireland v Retallack* [2011] NSWSC 846; 6 A.S.T.L.R. 585 where a gift of land owned by a company in which the testator owned 99.9 per cent of the shares was held effective.

(d) The Doctrine of Conversion

23–025 FN 118. DELETE TEXT FOR FOOTNOTE 118 AND REPLACE WITH THE FOLLOWING TEXT:

See further Snell (32nd edn) 6–008.

2.—THE MEANING OF CERTAIN WORDS DESCRIBING THINGS

(a) Money

Money has several meanings

23–045 FN 182. ADD AT END OF CURRENT FOOTNOTE TEXT:

Turner v Wall 1 A.S.T.L.R. 411.

(c) Personal Chattels, and Items Generally Included within that Description

Contents of a house

23–069 ADD AFTER SECOND PARAGRAPH:

Where a gift of a house, household goods, a motorcar and £10,000 was expressed to 'include any manuscripts scores and musical literary or other written material', there being no such items at the testator's house, all such items as the testator owned passed notwithstanding that they were located elsewhere: *Day v Harris*.[324a]

[324a] [2013] EWCA Civ 191; [2013] W.T.L.R. 591; 16 I.T.E.L.R. 111 at [101]–[108].

(d) Gifts of Original Papers, Pictures, Recordings etc. and Copyrights Therein

23–072 ADD NEW FN 333a AT THE END OF THE FIRST SENTENCE:

[333a] See 23–066 above.

CHAPTER 24

DESCRIPTION OF BENEFICIARIES: GENERAL

2.—GIFTS TO PARTICULAR PEOPLE

Identification of person inaccurately described

REPLACE THE LAST FOUR WORDS OF THE LAST PARAGRAPH "my **24–011**
nephew Mark Parkinson" WITH:

a great-nephew, as "my nephew Mark Parkinson".[41]

FN 41. DELETE FULLSTOP AT END OF FOOTNOTE AND ADD:

, approving the passage which is now para.1–17 of *Williams, Mortimer &*
Sunnucks, 'Executors, Administrators and Probate' (20th edn).

Clauses of inclusion or exclusion with names left blank

ADD AT END OF FIRST PARAGRAPH: **24–018**

A gift to a class but "the individual names of whom will be shown in a list to be
supplied later on" is void for uncertainty where no such list is found: *Public*
Trustee v Butler.[65a] Indeed, even if such a list had been found, it is submitted that
it would not have been admissible unless it had been executed as a will: see
Chapter 5 above.

[65a] [2012] EWHC 858 (Ch), [2012] W.T.L.R. 1043 at [14].

CHAPTER 25

DESCRIPTION OF BENEFICIARIES: RELATIONSHIPS

2.—GIFT TO SPOUSE OR CIVIL PARTNER OF ANOTHER

Divorced spouse or former civil partner

ADD AFTER FIRST PARAGRAPH: **25–008**

In the Bermudan case of *Guardian Ltd v Bermuda Trust Co Ltd*,[30a] the same rule
was held to apply to exclude the widows from a class of spouses, in the context
of a lifetime settlement, distinguishing *Greenwold v Greenwold*.[30b]

[30a] [2009] SC Bda 54 Civ; 15 I.T.E.L.R. 173.
[30b] [2008] EWHC 820 (Ch) (unreported).

10.—"RELATIONS"

ADD AT BEGINNING OF PARAGRAPH: **25–019**

A gift to a class of 'relations' is not inherently uncertain: see *Public Trustee v
Butler*[100a] where the following text was cited with approval.

[100a] [2012] EWHC 858 (Ch); [2012] W.T.L.R. 1043 at [18].

CHAPTER 26

DESCRIPTION OF BENEFICIARIES: CHILDREN

2.—ILLEGITIMATE CHILDREN AT COMMON LAW (WILL EXECUTED BEFORE JANUARY 1, 1970)

Legitimacy

FN 16. AT THE END OF CURRENT FOOTNOTE TEXT, DELETE "Dicey and Morris, 17–026 and following." AND REPLACE WITH:

26–004

Dicey, Morris and Collins, *The Conflict of Laws*, 15th edn (2012), 17–028.

Presumption of marriage

FN 22. AT THE END OF CURRENT FOOTNOTE TEXT, DELETE "Dicey and Morris, 17–037 and following." AND REPLACE WITH:

26–005

Dicey, Morris and Collins, *The Conflict of Laws*, 15th edn (2012), 17–039.

Presumption of legitimacy

FN 26. ADD AT END OF CURRENT FOOTNOTE TEXT:

26–006

The reference to Cretney is now to 17–006.

5.—LEGITIMATED CHILDREN

Effects of legitimation on death after 1926 and before 1976

(a) *Death after legitimation.*

FN 138. ADD AT END OF CURRENT FOOTNOTE TEXT:

26–035

But compare *Re The Erskine Trust, Gregg v Pigott* [2012] EWHC 732 (Ch); [2013] Ch. 135; [2012] W.T.L.R. 953, referred to at para.26–050a, below, for adopted children.

6.—ADOPTED CHILDREN

ADD NEW PARAGRAPH 26–050a DIRECTLY BELOW HEADING
"6.—ADOPTED CHILDREN":

*The European Convention on Human Rights 1950 and the Human Rights Act
1998*

26–050a　The law as explained in this section relating to adopted children is affected by the Convention and the Act, because of the right to family life given in art.8 of the Convention, and the prohibition on discrimination in art.14. In some cases, adopted children may be entitled to take under a will by virtue of these articles, even though they would not otherwise be entitled. In *Re The Erskine 1948 Trust, Gregg v Pigott,*[176a] Mark Herbert QC sitting as a Deputy Judge of the Chancery Division was able to construe a settlement made in 1948 to enable adopted children to take, because of certain special features he found to exist. He did so in the light of the guidance he found in the decision of the European Court of Human Rights in *Pla v Andorra,*[176b] that (1) the court had to avoid a decision which was unreasonable, arbitrary or blatantly inconsistent with the prohibition on discrimination in art.14; (2) the disposition had to be construed in a way which corresponded to national law and the Convention; and (3) effect had to be given to any distinction which the disposition made between biological and adopted children. The implications of this decision still have to be fully explored.

[176a] [2012] EWHC 732 (Ch); [2013] Ch. 135; [2012] W.T.L.R. 953.
[176b] [2004] F.C.R. 630.

Death on or after January 1, 1976

(a) *General rule.*

26–065　ADD AT THE END OF THE PARAGRAPH:

Clause 4 of the Inheritance and Trustees' Powers Bill will, if enacted, preserve the contingent interest of a child who is adopted after it comes into force, unless the contingent interest is an interest in remainder. It is also, of course, possible for a parent to leave property to his natural child who has been adopted, by using sufficiently clear words: *Hardy v Hardy.*[203a]

[203a] [2013] EWHC 83 (Ch).

11.—DISTRIBUTION PER CAPITA AND PER STIRPES

Distribution per capita

26–085　FN 301. ADD AT END OF CURRENT FOOTNOTE TEXT:

Spurling v Broadhurst [2012] W.T.L.R. 1813.

CHAPTER 27

DESCRIPTION OF BENEFICIARIES: CLASS GIFTS

1.—GENERAL PRINCIPLES

27–001 FN 1. AT END OF FOONOTE DELETE "Parry and Clark" AND REPLACE WITH THE FOLLOWING TEXT:

Parry & Kerridge

Release or disclaimer of life interest

27–008 FN 31. ADD AT END OF CURRENT FOOTNOTE TEXT:

The Australian and Hong Kong courts have preferred the reasoning in the earlier cases, and held that the class closes on acceleration: *Bassett v Bassett* [2003] NSWSC 691; [2005] W.T.L.R. 51; *Hamersley v Newton* [2005] WASC 221; 8 I.T.E.L.R. 256; *Re Sadick, da Silva v HSBC Trustee (Hong Kong) Ltd* [2009] HKCU 1957; [2010] W.T.L.R. 873.

CHAPTER 28

DESCRIPTIONS OF INTERESTS

1.—ABSOLUTE INTERESTS

(a) No Words Needed to Pass an Absolute Interest

(iii) *Further gifts of the same property*

ADD NEW FOOTNOTE 5a AT END OF FIRST SENTENCE: **28–005**

The same approach was taken in construing a lifetime settlement in *Bindra v Chopra* [2009] EWCA Civ 203; [2009] W.T.L.R. 781.

(e) Effect of Subsequent Restrictions Upon Absolute Interests

Absolute gift remains if subsequent restrictions fail

ADD AFTER THIRD PARAGRAPH: **28–017**

In *Webb v Oldfield* [2012] EWHC 3469 (Ch), a will provided first that the testator wanted "A's money protected by the discretion of my executors in view of addiction", and then left A a one-third share of residue "absolutely". The former words, given their lack of clarity and the absence of any other beneficiaries or gift over, were held insufficient to displace the normal meaning of 'absolutely'.

(f) Gifts Beneficial or in Trust

(ii) *Trust inferred from precatory words*

FN 75. AT END OF FOOTNOTE DELETE "Snell, 30th edn, 20–019 and   **28–022** following." AND REPLACE WITH:

See Snell, 32nd edn, 22–014.

ADD AT END OF PENULTIMATE PARAGRAPH:

In *Webb v Oldfield*,[97a] the words "I want A's money protected by the discretion of my executors" were treated as merely precatory, and did not prevent A having an absolute interest.

[97a] [2012] EWHC 3469 (Ch).

3.—ESTATES FOR LIFE AND PUR AUTRE VIE

(a) Creation of Life Estates

(ii) *Effect of gift at the death of first taker*

28–069   FN 241. DELETE FOOTNOTE TEXT AND REPLACE WITH FOLLOWING TEXT:

Sherratt v Bentley (1843) 2 M. & K. 149; *Hare v Westropp* (1861) 9 W.R. 689; *Brook's Will, Re* (1865) 2 Dr. & Sm. 362; *Bagshaw's Trusts, Re* (1877) 46 L.J. Ch. 567; *Lupton, in the estate of* [1905] P. 321.

(iii) *Gift of what remains*

28–070   FN 252. ADD AFTER FIRST SENTENCE IN FOOTNOTE:

See also *Bindra v Chopra* [2009] EWCA Civ 203; [2009] W.T.L.R. 781 where the court cut down the apparent effect of an earlier provision in order to give effect to the later.

(c) Provisions Determining Life Interests

28–080   ADD AT END OF SECOND PARAGRAPH:

A provision referring to the income from a particular property until sold was not treated as limiting the interest to the income prior to sale or as causing the interest to determine on sale: *Beard v Shadler*.[287a]

[287a] [2011] EWHC 114 (Ch); [2011] W.T.L.R. 1147 at [22].

CHAPTER 29

CONDITIONS

3.—VOID CONDITIONS

(b) Uncertainty

Condition subsequent

FN 38. ADD AT END OF CURRENT FOOTNOTE TEXT: **29–012**

This statement of the law was applied by the Grand Court of the Cayman Islands in relation to an *inter vivos* settlement in *AN v Barclays Private Bank and Trust (Cayman) Ltd* (2006) 9 I.T.E.L.R. 630. A forfeiture on a challenge to the validity of the trust was sufficiently certain, but one on a challenge to decisions of the trustees was not.

(d) Repugnant Conditions

ADD NEW SUB-SECTION "viii" AND NEW PARAGRAPH AFTER **29–022**
PARAGRAPH 29–022:

(viii) *Conditions that would make trust/will unenforceable*

In *AN v Barclays Private Bank and Trust (Cayman) Ltd*,[96a] a case concerning an **29–022a**
inter vivos settlement, the Grand Court held that a clause which purported to forfeit the interest of any beneficiary who challenged any decision by a trustee was to be construed so that they would not shut out a challenge "based on probable cause or good faith or which are not taken merely frivolously and vexatiously or without good reason", even if ultimately unsuccessful. A wider construction would impinge upon the "irreducible core of obligations owed by the trustees" (*per* Millett LJ in *Armitage v Nurse*[96b]) making the trust unenforceable, which would be repugnant and amount to an ouster of the court's jurisdiction.

[96a] (2006) 9 I.T.E.L.R. 630.
[96b] [1998] Ch. 241 at 253.

6.—CONDITIONS TO ASSUME A NAME, TITLE OR ARMS

FN 127. ADD AT END OF CURRENT FOOTNOTE TEXT: **29–031**

For the recent resumption of this dispute, see *Howard v Howard-Lawson* [2012] EWCA Civ 6; [2012] W.T.L.R. 617

ADD AT END OF SIXTH PARAGRAPH:

A condition to "apply for and endeavour to obtain the Royal Licence" to bear certain arms was satisfied by applying to the College of Arms for permission to adopt the arms even though the petition for a Royal Licence was not lodged until after the period allowed by the will: *Howard v Howard-Lawson*.[144a]

[144a] [2012] EWCA Civ 6; [2012] W.T.L.R. 617.

8.—CONDITIONS NOT TO DISPUTE A WILL

29–039   FN 199. ADD AT END OF CURRENT FOOTNOTE TEXT:

See the extensive summary of the law in the judgment of Smellie C.J. in *AN v Barclays Private Bank and Trust (Cayman) Ltd* (2006) 9 I.T.E.L.R. 630 (Cayman Islands).

FN 200. ADD AT END OF CURRENT FOOTNOTE TEXT:

A similar conclusion was reached in the case of an *inter vivos* settlement in the Cayman Islands case of *AN v Barclays Private Bank and Trust (Cayman) Ltd* (2006) 9 I.T.E.L.R. 630.

CHAPTER 30

VESTING

1.—INTRODUCTION

FN 1. ADD AT END OF CURRENT FOOTNOTE TEXT: **30–001**

For a recent Australian consideration of vesting, see *Fairbairn v Vavaressos* [2010] NSWCA 234; 13 I.T.E.L.R. 478.

FN 4. ADD AT END OF CURRENT FOOTNOTE TEXT:

Legacies can be varied under the Variation of Trusts Act 1958: *Re Bernstein* [2008] EWHC 3454 (Ch); [2010] W.T.L.R. 559.

Chapter 31

PERPETUITY AND ACCUMULATION

5.—The 2009 Act and its Effect

ADD NEW FN 255a TO THE END OF THE HEADING "5.—The 2009 Act **31–060** and its Effect":

255a In *Pitt v Holt* [2013] 2 W.L.R. 1200, Lord Walker giving the judgment of the court noted that thanks to the succession of Acts discussed in this chapter, "the rule against perpetuities has lost its terrors" (at [15]).

Chapter 34

ADMINISTRATION

1.—Introduction

Administration of Estates Act 1925

FN 1. DELETE "50–40." AT THE END OF CURRENT FOOTNOTE TEXT AND ADD AFTER "Williams, Mortimer and Sunnucks,": **34–001**

Executors, Administrators and Probate, 20th edn (2013), Ch.51.

2.—The Order of Assets

Statutory order of application of assets

FN 3. DELETE "49–02 onwards." AT THE END OF CURRENT FOOTNOTE TEXT AND ADD AFTER "Williams, Mortimer and Sunnucks,": **34–002**

20th edn, Ch.49.

3.—Payment of Legacies

(a) Out of What Property Legacies are Payable

Rules before 1926

FN 41. DELETE CURRENT FOOTNOTE AND ADD NEW TEXT: **34–008**

See generally E. C. Ryder, [1956] C.L.J. 80; Parry and Kerridge: *The Law of Succession*, 22–01 and following; Williams, Mortimer and Sunnucks, 20th edn, Ch.75.

5.—PROPERTY SUBJECT TO A CHARGE

Real Estate Charges Acts

34–026   FN 117. DELETE "50–11 and following." AT THE END OF CURRENT FOOTNOTE TEXT AND ADD AFTER "Williams, Mortimer and Sunnucks,":

20th edn, 51–11. For a recent case see *Re the Estate of Romona Ross, Petterson v Ross* [2013] EWHC 2724 (Ch).

7.—MARSHALLING

34–034   FN 148. ADD AT END OF CURRENT FOOTNOTE TEXT:

For a recent case, see *Re the Estate of Romona Ross, Petterson v Ross* [2013] EWHC 2724 (Ch).

CHAPTER 35

ADMINISTRATIVE POWERS OF TRUSTEES

5.—POWER TO CARRY ON TESTATOR'S BUSINESS

FN 96. DELETE "55–85 and following." AT THE END OF CURRENT
FOOTNOTE TEXT AND ADD AFTER "Williams, Mortimer and
Sunnucks,":

35–026

20th edn, 57–87 and following.

6.—POWER OF MAINTENANCE

FN 101. DELETE "Snell, 26–37 and following;" AND REPLACE WITH:

35–027

Snell, 32nd edn (2011), 28–037 and following;

7.—POWER OF ADVANCEMENT

FN 125. DELETE "Snell, 26–44 and following;" AND REPLACE WITH:

35–033

Snell, 32nd edn, 28–046 and following;

8.—DISCRETIONARY POWERS GENERALLY

When the court will interfere

FN 165. DELETE "Snell, 27–28;". ADD AT END OF FOOTNOTE:

35–036

Snell, 32nd edn (2011), 29–001 and following. It should be noted that the
jurisdiction of the court under the Variation of Trusts Act 1958 applies to
property held by personal representatives: *Re Bernstein* [2008] EWHC 3454;
[2010] W.T.L.R. 559.

ADD NEW PARAGRAPHS AFTER THE LAST PARAGRAPH:

The Supreme Court has now given an authoritative explanation of the Rule, and
the related jurisdiction to set aside a transaction on the ground of mistake: *Futter*

v Futter; Pitt v Holt.[176a] In summary (and the judgment of Lord Walker needs careful study), if an exercise by trustees of a discretionary power is within the terms of the power, but the trustees have in some way breached their duties in respect of that exercise, then the trustees' act is not void, but it may be voidable at the instance of a beneficiary who is adversely affected. Whether or not the court avoids it depends on equitable defences, and the discretion of the court.

As for mistake, the court must consider in the round the existence of a distinct mistake, its degree of centrality to the transaction, and the seriousness of its consequences. Having done that, it must make an evaluative judgment whether it would be unconscionable, or unjust, to leave the mistake uncorrected.

[176a] [2013] UKSC 26; [2013] 2 W.L.R. 1200.

9.—POWER OF APPROPRIATION

35–038   FN 181. DELETE "Williams, Mortimer and Sunnucks, 54–54 and following; Snell, 33–10 and following;" AND REPLACE WITH:

Williams, Mortimer and Sunnucks, 20th edn, 55–54; Snell, 32nd edn, 35–010;

FN 181. ADD AT END OF FOOTNOTE:

The power ought to be broadly construed in a way that promotes practical and convenient trust administration: *Hughes v Bourne* [2012] EWHC 2232 (Ch); [2012] W.T.L.R. 1333.

10.—POWER TO CHARGE FOR PROFESSIONAL SERVICES

35–041   FN 194. DELETE CURRENT FOOTNOTE AND REPLACE WITH:

Williams, Mortimer and Sunnucks, 20th edn, Ch.56; Lewin, 20–141 and following; Snell, 32nd edn, 7–042. See Williams, Mortimer and Sunnucks and Lewin on Trusts (18th edn) generally for other principles relating to the costs of personal representatives and trustees.

CHAPTER 36

RULES AGAINST DOUBLE PORTIONS AND OTHER DOUBLE PROVISION

2.—SATISFACTION

(a) Cases of Double Portions

Meaning of portion

FN 6. ADD AT END OF FOOTNOTE: **36–002**

The summary of the law from this decision was applied in *Re Frost, deceased* [2013] EWHC 435 (Ch); [2013] W.T.L.R. 673.

FN 9. ADD AT END OF FOOTNOTE:

Re Frost, deceased [2013] EWHC 435 (Ch); [2013] W.T.L.R. 673.

3.—ADEMPTION

(a) Ademption of Portions

Differences between property willed and given

FN 109. ADD AT END OF FOOTNOTE: **36–026**

But this is not a rule of law: *Race v Race* [2002] EWHC 1868 (Ch); [2002] W.T.L.R. 1193, cited at 36–019, above.

CHAPTER 37

ADEMPTION

Gifts by the testator during his life

FN 22. ADD AT END OF THE CURRENT FOOTNOTE TEXT:　　　　　**37–006**

In this connection, a gift may be ineffective by reason of undue influence: *Aldridge v Turner* [2004] EWHC 2768 (Ch); *Hart v Burbidge* [2013] EWHC 1628 (Ch); [2013] W.T.L.R. 1191.

Conversion by lawful authority

FN 31. DELETE "*Banks v National Westminster Bank* [2006] W.T.L.R.　　**37–009** 11693;" AND REPLACE WITH FOLLOWING TEXT:

Banks v National Westminster Bank [2006] W.T.L.R. 1693;

FN 32. DELETE "See also above, para.37–009." AND REPLACE WITH FOLLOWING TEXT:

See also fn.31, above.

Chapter 38

INCOME OR INTEREST CARRIED BY GIFTS

2.—What is Income of Specific Gift?—Apportionment

Apportionment Act

ADD AT END OF PARAGRAPH: **38–011**

The Bill was enacted on January 31, 2013. Its provisions only apply to trusts created after it came into force on October 1, 2013, so the old law remains important.

CHAPTER 39

RIGHTS BETWEEN TENANT FOR LIFE AND REMAINDERMAN

1.—INTRODUCTION

ADD AFTER END OF SECOND PARAGRAPH: **39–001**

The Bill was enacted on January 31, 2013. Its provisions only apply to trusts created after it came into force on October 1, 2013, so the old law remains important.

CHAPTER 40

PROFESSIONAL NEGLIGENCE

FN 1. ADD AT THE END OF THE CURRENT FOOTNOTE: **40–001**

These texts deal with professional negligence by and in relation to executors. For a recent case where such a claim was time barred, see *Lane v Cullens* [2011] EWHC Civ 547.

5.—BREACH OF DUTY

Unreasonable delay in preparation of will or in progress of claim

ADD TO END OF FIRST PARAGRAPH: **40–020**

In *Feltham v Freer Bouskell*,[88a] a solicitor had doubts as to the testatrix's capacity, and sought a medical opinion before accepting instructions to draft a will. It was held that it was part of a solicitor's obligation in such circumstances to chase up the doctor if he did not receive a report in good time, and/or to instruct a new doctor if the person originally instructed could not report swiftly. The solicitor on belatedly receiving the report still had concerns, and so decided to do nothing—i.e. not to prepare a will. That the testatrix's granddaughter, at the request of the testatrix, prepared the will herself was a direct consequence of the breach of duty by the solicitor, and not an answer to it.

[88a] [2013] EWHC 1952.

Failure to protect estate from an unnecessary charge to tax

ADD TO END OF PARAGRAPH: **40–023**

In relation to other forms of tax, the Court of Appeal held in *Swain Mason v Mills & Reeve*[109a] that a firm of solicitors was not under a duty to advise on the adverse tax consequences that would arise on the death of a client shortly after completion of a management buy-out where he had not asked for advice and the death occurred during a medical procedure which was routine and which the solicitors knew of essentially by chance.

[109a] [2012] EWCA Civ 498; [2012] W.T.L.R. 1827.

Failure to take adequate instructions, to ensure testator fully understands
legal effect of dispositions he proposes to make, or adequately to advise

40–025   ADD TO END OF LAST PARAGRAPH:

In *Hill v Fellowes Solicitors LLP*,[132a] an allegation was made that a solicitor had breached his duty of care by, inter alia, acting for the testator without proper instructions, as the testator was suffering from dementia. The claim was dismissed. It was held that there was no evidence that the solicitor had known that the client was suffering from dementia or ought to have appreciated that this was the position. It was held by Sharp J. that a solicitor was generally only required to make inquiries as to a person's capacity to contract if there were circumstances such as to raise that doubt in the mind of a reasonably competent practitioner. Further, there was plainly no duty upon solicitors in general to obtain medical evidence on every occasion upon which they were instructed by an elderly client just in case they lacked capacity: such a requirement would be insulting and unnecessary.

[132a] [2011] P.N.L.R. 13.

INDEX